W9-AWC-496

**PRACTICE
MAKES
PERFECT**

Exploring Grammar

PRACTICE
MAKES
PERFECT

Exploring Grammar

Gary Robert Muschla

New York   Chicago   San Francisco   Lisbon   London   Madrid   Mexico City
Milan   New Delhi   San Juan   Seoul   Singapore   Sydney   Toronto

The **McGraw·Hill** Companies

Copyright © 2011 by Gary Robert Muschla. All rights reserved. Printed in the United
States of America. Except as permitted under the United States Copyright Act of 1976,
no part of this publication may be reproduced or distributed in any form or by any
means, or stored in a database or retrieval system, without the prior written permission
of the publisher.

A version of this book was previously published under the title *Teach Terrific Grammar,
Grades 4–5*.

7 8 9 10 11 12 QVS/QVS 20 19 18 17 16

ISBN 978-0-07-174548-2
MHID   0-07-174548-3

Library of Congress Control Number: 2010926961

Trademarks: McGraw-Hill, the McGraw-Hill Publishing logo, Practice Makes Perfect,
and related trade dress are trademarks or registered trademarks of The McGraw-Hill
Companies and/or its affiliates in the United States and other countries and may not
be used without written permission. All other trademarks are the property of their
respective owners. The McGraw-Hill Companies is not associated with any product or
vendor mentioned in this book.

McGraw-Hill books are available at special quantity discounts to use as premiums and
sales promotions or for use in corporate training programs. To contact a representative,
please e-mail us at bulksales@mcgraw-hill.com.

This book is printed on acid-free paper.

For Judy and Erin, as always.

Contents

ix

Contents

About This Book

Most students find the rules of English grammar to be confusing if not outright overwhelming. Adding to the muddle are the many exceptions to the rules that are just plain maddening. But understanding grammar is essential for students to speak and write with competence and clarity.

Practice Makes Perfect: Exploring Grammar can be a valuable resource in learning grammar. It can be used by both students and teachers. Students (working alone or with their parents) can complete the worksheets, while teachers will find the materials of the book to be useful for classroom instruction. Tip sheets throughout the book highlight grammatical facts and rules, while self-correcting worksheets provide students with an interesting way to learn and practice grammar skills.

Learning grammar is challenging. It is my hope that this book will make the study of grammar an enjoyable and successful experience.

About This Book

How to Use This Book

Practice Makes Perfect: Exploring Grammar is divided into nine parts. Each part concentrates on grammar skills and includes tip sheets and worksheets. An answer key for the worksheets is included at the end of the book.

Part 1 "Sentences" includes three tip sheets and seventeen worksheets that focus on sentence types, sentence structure, subjects, predicates, fragments, and run-on sentences. In addition, four review worksheets are included at the end of Part 1.

Part 2 "Nouns" includes four tip sheets and ten worksheets that focus on singular nouns, plural nouns, common nouns, proper nouns, irregular plural nouns, and possessive nouns. Part 2 concludes with four review worksheets.

Part 3 "Verbs" contains nine tip sheets and twenty-five worksheets that cover action verbs, verb phrases, linking verbs, direct objects, nouns and adjectives that follow linking verbs, contractions with verbs, tenses, subject-verb agreement, and irregular verbs. Four review worksheets conclude this part of the book.

Part 4 "Pronouns" contains six tip sheets and fifteen worksheets on personal pronouns, subject pronouns, object pronouns, possessive pronouns, contractions with pronouns, and antecedents. Three review worksheets are also included.

Part 5 "Adjectives" contains three tip sheets and seven worksheets on identifying adjectives, proper adjectives, and the comparison of adjectives. Two review worksheets conclude Part 5.

Part 6 "Adverbs" includes three tip sheets and eight worksheets on identifying adverbs, the comparison of adverbs, and double negatives. Part 6 also includes three review worksheets.

Part 7 "Prepositions, Conjunctions, and Interjections" contains four tip sheets and ten worksheets on prepositions, prepositional phrases, objects of prepositions, conjunctions, and interjections. Part 7 ends with four review worksheets.

Part 8 "Punctuation and Capitalization" contains eight tip sheets and twenty-three worksheets on end punctuation, commas, colons, hyphens, apostrophes, quotation marks, italics, and capitalization. Eleven review worksheets are also included.

Part 9 "Usage and Proofreading" contains one tip sheet and four worksheets on common words that cause confusion, and one tip sheet and ten worksheets on proofreading to find grammatical mistakes.

The tip sheets and worksheets throughout the book are designed to make learning grammar easier. Each tip sheet serves as a resource, providing facts and information about topics and skills in grammar. The worksheets have easy-to-follow directions and require no additional materials. You may want to check the tip sheets if you need help in completing the worksheets. The worksheets are self-correcting. You are presented with a trivia-type question at the top of the worksheet, which you can answer by completing the worksheet correctly.

The skills covered in this book follow the typical language arts and grammar curriculum for grades 4–5. The skill or topic addressed in each worksheet is included with the number and title of the worksheet in the table of contents. The table of contents therefore serves as a skills list.

You will find that some skills and topics are addressed by two, three, or more worksheets. In such cases, the worksheets progress in degree of difficulty from basic to more challenging—the first worksheet of the set being designated by 1, the second by 2, the third by 3, and so on.

The tip sheets and worksheets throughout this book offer 206 separate activities. They offer a variety of exercises that will help you gain a greater understanding of grammar.

PART 1

Sentences

A sentence is an arrangement of words that expresses a complete thought. Sentences are the foundation of communication in English.

The tip sheets and worksheets in this part focus on sentences. One tip sheet and Worksheets 1.1 through 1.3 focus on sentence kinds and structures. One tip sheet and Worksheets 1.4 through 1.14 concentrate on subjects and predicates. The final tip sheet and Worksheets 1.15 through 1.17 concentrate on fragments and run-on sentences, while Worksheets 1.18 through 1.21 review sentences.

Kinds and Structures of Sentences

Sentences may be one of four kinds:

1. A *declarative* sentence makes a statement. It ends with a period.

   The game begins at seven.

2. An *interrogative* sentence asks a question. It ends with a question mark.

   Did you finish your homework?

3. An *imperative* sentence gives an order or asks someone to do something. It ends with a period.

   Please answer the phone.

4. An *exclamatory* sentence shows strong emotion. It ends with an exclamation point.

   Watch out!

Sentences have different structures. Here are two of the most common:

- A *simple* sentence has one complete subject and one complete predicate.

  Manuel plays the drums.

- A *compound* sentence contains two or more simple sentences joined by a conjunction such as *and, but,* or *or.* A comma usually comes before the conjunction.

  Sara has brown hair, but her brother has blond hair.

© Gary Robert Muschla

1.1 E. B. White

E. B. White was the author of *Charlotte's Web*. What do the initials *E. B.* stand for?

To answer the question, label each sentence below as *declarative, interrogative, imperative*, or *exclamatory*. Select your answers from the choices after each sentence. Write the letter of each answer in the space above its sentence number at the bottom of the page. The first letter is given.

1. E. B. White was born in Mount Vernon, New York, in 1899.
   N. Declarative   R. Interrogative   D. Imperative   W. Exclamatory

2. He wrote many books for children.
   R. Declarative   O. Interrogative   A. Imperative   T. Exclamatory

3. Do you know that he wrote *Stuart Little*?
   R. Declarative   **W. Interrogative**   N. Imperative   J. Exclamatory

4. Please hand me that book on the shelf.
   M. Declarative   I. Interrogative   **S. Imperative**   L. Exclamatory

5. He also wrote *The Trumpet of the Swan*.
   B. Declarative   U. Interrogative   H. Imperative   Y. Exclamatory

6. That's a great book!
   H. Declarative   L. Interrogative   A. Imperative   **K. Exclamatory**

7. Isn't *Charlotte's Web* one of the most popular children's books of all time?
   T. Declarative   **L. Interrogative**   U. Imperative   E. Exclamatory

8. E. B. White is one of my favorite authors.
   O. Declarative   D. Interrogative   N. Imperative   E. Exclamatory

9. Check the Internet for more information on E. B. White.
   S. Declarative   A. Interrogative   **Y. Imperative**   M. Exclamatory

E L W Y N   B R O O K S
   7 3 9 1   5 2 8 8 6 4

© Gary Robert Muschla

1.2 Special States

The biggest state in the United States is Alaska. What is the smallest state?

To answer the question, name each sentence below. Select your answers from the choices after each sentence. Write the letter of each answer in the space above its sentence number at the bottom of the page. You will need to divide the letters into words.

1. Kim's favorite subject in school is geography.
   S. Simple   N. Compound

2. She likes learning about different places and people.
   E. Simple   A. Compound

3. Kim knows a lot about the states, and she plans to visit each one someday.
   O. Simple   A. Compound

4. At one time our country had only thirteen states, but today there are fifty.
   T. Simple   I. Compound

5. Alaska and Hawaii were the last two states to join the Union.
   O. Simple   G. Compound

6. Texas was once the biggest state, but now Alaska is the biggest.
   G. Simple   L. Compound

7. Canada is north of the United States, and Mexico is south of our country.
   E. Simple   N. Compound

8. Alaska is separated from the lower forty-eight states by Canada.
   D. Simple   J. Compound

9. Canada is larger than the United States, but it has a smaller population.
   N. Simple   R. Compound

10. Kim would like to travel around the world someday.
    H. Simple   E. Compound

$$\frac{R}{9} \quad \frac{H}{10} \quad \frac{O}{5} \quad \frac{D}{8} \quad \frac{e}{2} \quad \frac{I}{4} \quad \frac{S}{1} \quad \frac{L}{6} \quad \frac{a}{3} \quad \frac{n}{7} \quad \frac{d}{8}$$

© Gary Robert Muschla

1.3 A Space First

This woman was the first African American woman to travel in space. Who was she?

To answer the question, name each sentence below. Select your answers from the choices after each sentence. Write the letter of each answer in the space above its sentence number at the bottom of the page.

1. Astronauts are space travelers and explorers.
   E. Simple   I. Compound

2. Many astronauts are pilots, but others are scientists.
   K. Simple   A. Compound

3. Astronauts spend many hours training.
   N. Simple   I. Compound

4. Flying in space is exciting, but it is also dangerous.
   C. Simple   J. Compound

5. Accidents have happened, and lives have been lost.
   E. Simple   M. Compound

6. On May 5, 1961, Alan Shepard became the first American to fly in space.
   I. Simple   E. Compound

7. On July 20, 1969, Neil Armstrong became the first human to walk on the moon.
   O. Simple   W. Compound

8. Other trips to the moon followed, and scientists learned much about the moon.
   N. Simple   S. Compound

9. Scientists dream of visiting Mars, but that mission is many years away.
   H. Simple   M. Compound

10. Someday human beings will travel throughout the stars.
    E. Simple   I. Compound

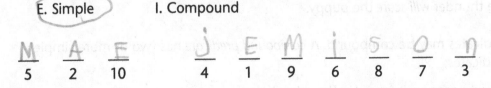

M   A   E   J   E   M   i   S   O   n
5   2   10   4   1   9   6   8   7   3

© Gary Robert Muschla

TIP SHEET

Subjects and Predicates

Sentences are built around subjects and predicates.

- The *complete subject* of a sentence includes all the words that tell who the subject is or what it is about.

  Tara is a piano teacher.

  The powerful earthquake caused much damage.

  The thunder will scare the puppy.

- The *simple subject* is the most important word or words in the complete subject. The simple subject is usually a noun or pronoun.

  Tara is a piano teacher.

  The powerful *earthquake* caused much damage.

  The *thunder* will scare the puppy.

- Subjects may be compound. A *compound subject* has two or more simple subjects.

  Jason and *Joanna* are cousins.

- The *complete predicate* of a sentence includes all the words that tell what the subject is or does.

  Tara *is a piano teacher.*

  The powerful earthquake *caused much damage.*

  The thunder *will scare the puppy.*

- The *simple predicate* is the most important word or words in the complete predicate. It is a verb or a verb phrase.

  Tara *is* a piano teacher.

  The powerful earthquake *caused* much damage.

  The thunder *will scare* the puppy.

- Predicates may be compound. A *compound predicate* has two or more simple predicates.

  Roberta *sang* and *danced* in the school play.

© Gary Robert Muschla

1.4 A President's Ride in an Automobile

This president was the first to ride in an automobile. Who was he?

To answer the question, read each sentence below. Decide if the slash divides the sentence into its complete subject and complete predicate. If it does, write the letter for *yes* in the space above the sentence number at the bottom of the page. If the sentence is not divided correctly, write the letter for *no*.

1. The first automobiles / were called horseless carriages.
   S. Yes ⟵(circled)   K. No

2. Many inventors worked / on early automobiles.
   E. Yes   H. No ⟵(circled)

3. Henry Ford built one / of the first cars in 1893.
   S. Yes   D. No ⟵(circled)

4. Early cars / broke down often.
   E. Yes ⟵(circled)   O. No

5. Many people thought / of "motoring" as a sport.
   H. Yes   L. No ⟵(circled)

6. Many improvements in / automobiles were made.
   K. Yes   R. No ⟵(circled)

7. Soon people / looked upon automobiles as a means of transportation.
   T. Yes ⟵(circled)   G. No

8. Many companies / began making automobiles.
   V. Yes ⟵(circled)   F. No

9. Today many families / own more than one automobile.
   O. Yes ⟵(circled)   R. No

T H E O D O R E   R O O S E V E L T
7 2 4 9 3 9 6 4   6 9 9 1 4 8 4 5 7

© Gary Robert Muschla

1.5 First Settlement

An English settlement was founded in Virginia in 1607. What was the name of this settlement?

To answer the question, read each sentence below. Find the slash that divides the sentence into a complete subject and complete predicate. Write the letter that is below the correct slash in the space above the sentence number at the bottom of the page.

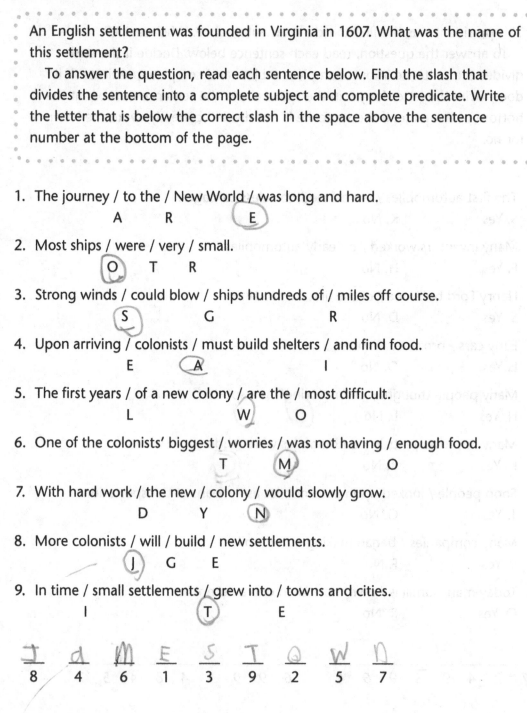

1. The journey / to the / New World / was long and hard.
        A   R   E

2. Most ships / were / very / small.
        O   T   R

3. Strong winds / could blow / ships hundreds of / miles off course.
         S   G   R

4. Upon arriving / colonists / must build shelters / and find food.
          E   A   I

5. The first years / of a new colony / are the / most difficult.
         L   W   O

6. One of the colonists' biggest / worries / was not having / enough food.
              T   M   O

7. With hard work / the new / colony / would slowly grow.
          D   Y   N

8. More colonists / will / build / new settlements.
           J   G   E

9. In time / small settlements / grew into / towns and cities.
      I   T   E

J A M E S T O W N
8 4 6 1 3 9 2 5 7

© Gary Robert Muschla

1.6 Hungry Toads

Toads are related to frogs, but toads spend more time on land. Scientists believe that toads eat a lot of insects during the summer. About how many insects might a single toad eat in one summer?

To answer the question, read each sentence below. Find the simple subject. Choose your answers from the underlined words. Write the letter that is below each simple subject in the space above its sentence number at the bottom of the page. You will need to divide the letters into words.

1. Toads are found in most parts of the world.
   O   A   N

2. Many people cannot tell the difference between a toad and a frog.
   R   A   L

3. Unlike frogs, toads usually live on land.
        A   H   U

4. A toad's skin is very rough.
   W   E   R

5. A toad's back legs are shorter than the back legs of frogs.
         U   L   J

6. Frogs can leap farther than toads.
   D   N   I

7. In the daytime, toads usually hide in dark, cool places.
       L   S   E

8. Most toads hunt insects at night.
   O   N   L

9. Toads hibernate during the winter.
   T   S   F

T   e   n   I   h   o   u   s   a   n   d
9   4   8   9   3   1   5   7   2   8   6

© Gary Robert Muschla

1.7 Above the South Pole

In 1929, this American explorer was the first man to fly over the South Pole. Who was he?

To answer the question, read the article below. Find the simple subject of each sentence. Start with the first sentence. Then write the letters beneath the simple subjects in order in the spaces at the bottom of the page.

The <u>South Pole</u> is in <u>Antarctica</u>. <u>Antarctica</u> is the <u>fifth</u> largest <u>continent</u> on the
      (R)   T   (I)   H   E

Earth. It is a <u>cold</u>, barren land. <u>Thick</u> ice covers most of Antarctica. <u>Even</u> in the
      (C)   O   M (H)   N

summer, Antarctica is extremely cold. <u>Only</u> a few <u>plants</u> grow in small ice-free <u>spots</u> far
    U   (A)   I   (R)   T

from the South Pole. The <u>temperature</u> on the <u>continent</u> is too cold for trees. <u>Penguins</u> are
            (D)   S   (B)

the <u>most</u> numerous <u>animals</u> in Antarctica. <u>Other</u> animals live in the <u>oceans</u> around the
    P   J   O   Y   V

continent. The <u>first</u> <u>explorers</u> did not reach Antarctica until the 1800s. <u>Today</u>, <u>scientists</u>
     N   R   S   D

carry out <u>research</u> in this icy land.
    N

R I C H A R D   B Y R D

© Gary Robert Muschla

1.8 Native American Explorer

In the early 1800s, Meriwether Lewis and William Clark explored the American west. A Native American woman helped them. Who was she?

To answer the question, read each sentence below. Find the simple predicates. Choose your answers from the underlined words. Write the letter beneath each simple predicate in the space above its sentence number at the bottom of the page.

1. In 1803, the United States bought a big area of land from France.
                    A   D   K

2. This land was the Louisiana Purchase.
      L   J   E

3. Thomas Jefferson asked Lewis and Clark to explore the land.
               E   C   S

4. In 1804, the explorers left St. Louis.
        U   E   C

5. They traveled westward through the wilderness.
         W   I   M

6. Finally, in 1805, they reached the Pacific.
      P   R   A

7. Lewis and Clark carefully mapped their journey.
            Y   A   N

8. They covered more than 8,000 miles.
     M   A   G

9. In time, the land of the Louisiana Purchase became several states.
         M   S   I

S	a	C	a	J	a	W	e	a
9	7	4	8	2	1	5	3	6

© Gary Robert Muschla

1.9 First Flight

Orville and Wilbur Wright were the first men to fly an airplane. Where in North Carolina did this first flight take place?

To answer the question, read the article below. Find the simple predicate in each sentence. Start with the first sentence. Then write the letters beneath the simple predicates in order in the spaces at the bottom of the page.

Wilbur and Orville Wright were brothers. At one time they repaired bicycles.
    J   K   S   O   I

But they wanted to fly. First they built gliders. A glider is an aircraft without an engine.
  H   T   S   T   Y   T   J

It glides with the wind. The Wright brothers learned much about flying from their
  H   O   A   L

gliders. Next, they designed a plane with a propeller. In 1903, Orville made the first
               W   R   K

powered airplane flight.
  N

K I T T Y   H A W K

© Gary Robert Muschla

1.10 Two of a Kind

Hawaii is one of only two states that have three consecutive vowels in its name (Hawaii). What is the other state?

To answer the question, read each sentence below. Find the simple subject and simple predicate. Match your answer with the possible answers that are given after each sentence. Only *one* of the possible answers for each sentence is correct. Write the letter that follows each correct answer in the space above its sentence number at the bottom of the page.

1. Josh's class learned about the states.
   Subject: states, S   Predicate: learned, A

2. The students discovered many interesting facts.
   Subject: students, S   Predicate: interesting, I

3. Fifty states belong to the United States.
   Subject: Fifty, N   Predicate: belong, I

4. Each state is special in its own way.
   Subject: state, A   Predicate: special, S

5. The thirteen colonies became the first thirteen states.
   Subject: thirteen, T   Predicate: became, I

6. Delaware was the first state to join the Union.
   Subject: Delaware, O   Predicate: first, U

7. Over the years, the country grew steadily.
   Subject: years, A   Predicate: grew, N

8. Settlers moved westward in search of new homes.
   Subject: Settlers, L   Predicate: search, M

9. In time, the country stretched across the continent.
   Subject: time, N   Predicate: stretched, U

L O U I S I A N A
8 6 9 5 2 3 1 7 4

© Gary Robert Muschla

1.11 The Biggest Turtle of All

This turtle can grow to weigh up to 1,300 pounds. It is thought to be the biggest turtle in the world. What kind of turtle is this?

To answer the question, read each sentence below. Find the simple subject and simple predicate. Match your answer with the possible answers that are given after each sentence. Only *one* of the possible answers for each sentence is correct. Write the letter that follows each correct answer in the space above its sentence number at the bottom of the page.

1. All turtles have hard shells.
   Subject: All, E   Predicate: have, H

2. A turtle's shell protects it from predators.
   Subject: shell, R   Predicate: from, T

3. Some turtles are only a few inches long.
   Subject: turtles, C   Predicate: only, K

4. Others grow to be several feet long.
   Subject: Others, T   Predicate: several, M

5. Some kinds of turtles weigh more than one thousand pounds.
   Subject: pounds, U   Predicate: weigh, B

6. Some turtles enjoy very long lives.
   Subject: Some, N   Predicate: enjoy, K

7. A few types live up to a hundred years.
   Subject: few, B   Predicate: live, L

8. All female turtles lay eggs.
   Subject: female, T   Predicate: lay, A

9. They bury their eggs in sand to keep them safe.
   Subject: They, E   Predicate: sand, L

$$\underset{7}{L}\ \underset{9}{e}\ \underset{8}{a}\ \underset{4}{T}\ \underset{1}{H}\ \underset{9}{e}\ \underset{2}{R}\ \underset{5}{B}\ \underset{8}{a}\ \underset{3}{C}\ \underset{6}{K}$$

© Gary Robert Muschla

1.12 American Flag Maker

Many people believe that this person made the first flag for the United States. What was this person's name?

To answer the question, read each sentence below. Decide if each sentence has a compound subject. If a compound subject is underlined correctly, write the letter for *correct* in the space above its sentence number at the bottom of the page. If a compound subject is not underlined correctly, write the letter for *incorrect*. You will need to divide the letters into words.

1. Selina and her group did a project on the Revolutionary War.
   O. Correct   S. Incorrect

2. Billy and Selina studied the causes of the war.
   S. Correct   T. Incorrect

3. Rachel, Alberto, and James read about important battles.
   E. Correct   A. Incorrect

4. Two students checked the Internet for information.
   E. Correct   S. Incorrect

5. All of the group members presented information to the class.
   I. Correct   Y. Incorrect

6. Many students asked excellent questions.
   R. Correct   T. Incorrect

7. Ahmed and Thomas learned much about George Washington.
   J. Correct   R. Incorrect

8. Jason and other students were curious about the Founding Fathers.
   B. Correct   N. Incorrect

9. Mrs. Carter, their teacher, was pleased with the project.
   E. Correct   S. Incorrect

$\underline{B}$ $\underline{e}$ $\underline{T}$ $\underline{S}$ $\underline{Y}$ $\underline{J}$ $\underline{o}$ $\underline{e}$ $\underline{S}$
8   3   6   2   5   7   1   4   9

© Gary Robert Muschla

1.13 Center of the Land

A monument marks the geographic center of the United States. This monument is in a pasture just northwest of this town. What is the name of the town, and in what state is it?

To answer the question, read each sentence below. Decide if the sentence has a compound predicate. If the compound predicate is underlined correctly, write the letter for *correct* in the space above its sentence number at the bottom of the page. If the compound predicate is not underlined correctly, write the letter for *incorrect*. You will need to divide the letters into words.

1. Amanda and her family went on a vacation last month.
   N. Correct   B. Incorrect

2. Before leaving, Amanda folded and packed her clothes.
   L. Correct   D. Incorrect

3. They drove from their home to a park in the mountains.
   N. Correct   K. Incorrect

4. The drive was long and tiring.
   I. Correct   E. Incorrect

5. Along the way, they stopped and ate lunch.
   O. Correct   M. Incorrect

6. They arrived at the park and found their campsite.
   A. Correct   C. Incorrect

7. The family walked to the lake and rented a canoe.
   N. Correct   G. Incorrect

8. Swimming and hiking were Amanda's favorite activities.
   N. Correct   S. Incorrect

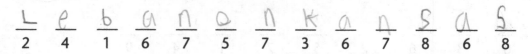

	L	e	b	a	n	o	n	K	a	n	s	a	s
	2	4	1	6	7	5	7	3	6	7	8	6	8

© Gary Robert Muschla

1.14 Passing Time

The average American does about four hours of this each day. What is it?

To answer the question, read each sentence below. Find the compound subject or compound predicate. Match your answers with the given possible answers. Only *one* of the possible answers for each sentence is correct. For most sentences, a compound subject (CS) *or* a compound predicate (CP) will be correct. For some sentences, neither is correct. Write the letter that follows each correct answer in the space above its sentence number at the bottom of the page. You will need to divide the letters into a word and the initials of a word.

1. Jonathan and James are brothers and best friends.
   CS: Jonathan, James, S   CP: are, best, U   Neither, O

2. They live in Smithton and go to Smithton Elementary School.
   CS: They, Smithton, C   CP: live, go, C   Neither, E

3. The two boys are members of a big family.
   CS: two, boys, R   CP: are, members, I   Neither, E

4. Of all the family members, Jonathan and James are most alike.
   CS: Jonathan, James, T   CP: are, alike, R   Neither, H

5. They read the same kinds of books and watch the same kinds of TV shows.
   CS: books, TV shows, E   CP: read, watch, A   Neither, I

6. The boys and their younger sister like sports.
   CS: boys, sister, H   CP: like, sports, L   Neither, N

7. Jenna, their younger sister, is an excellent softball player.
   CS: Jenna, sister, L   CP: is, excellent, F   Neither, W

8. Jessica, the oldest child, sings and dances in the school play each year.
   CS: Jessica, school, T   CP: sings, dances, V   Neither, C

9. Jessica hopes to be an actress someday.
   CS: Jessica, actress, S   CP: hopes, to, M   Neither, T

W	A	T	C	H	E	S	+	V
7	5	9	2	6	3	1	4	8

© Gary Robert Muschla

Fragments and Run-On Sentences

A complete sentence has a subject and a predicate. It expresses a complete thought. Sentence fragments and run-on sentences are incorrect sentences.

- A *fragment* is a group of words that make up only part of a sentence. A fragment does not express a complete thought. A fragment may be missing a subject, a predicate, or both.

  A birthday card to Anna.

  Listened to music.

  The cute kitten.

- To correct a fragment, rewrite it to form a complete sentence.

  I sent a birthday card to Anna.

  Alex listened to music.

  The cute kitten played with the toy mouse.

- A *run-on sentence* is made of two or more sentences that are joined incorrectly.

  The girls went shopping they rented a movie.

  The clown was funny, the audience laughed at his tricks.

- To correct a run-on sentence, write it as a compound sentence or as two separate sentences. You may also combine the ideas into one sentence.

  The girls went shopping, and they rented a movie.

  The girls went shopping. They rented a movie.

  The girls went shopping and rented a movie.

  The clown was funny, and the audience laughed at his tricks.

  The clown was funny. The audience laughed at his tricks.

© Gary Robert Muschla

1.15 Big Mouth

Sentences

After the whale, this animal has the biggest mouth of any mammal. What is it?

To answer the question, decide if each example below is a complete sentence or a sentence fragment. Write the letter of each answer in the space above the example's number at the bottom of the page.

1. Mammals are found all over the world.
   (T. Complete Sentence)   H. Fragment

2. Live on land and in rivers, lakes, and oceans.
   N. Complete Sentence   (S. Fragment)

3. Mammals are warm-blooded and have hair or fur.
   (I. Complete Sentence)   O. Fragment

4. Some mammals are very large.
   (M. Complete Sentence)   N. Fragment

5. Mice, for example, tiny mammals.
   E. Complete Sentence   (A. Fragment)

6. Whales are mammals, too.
   (O. Complete Sentence)   A. Fragment

7. But not all animals are mammals.
   (U. Complete Sentence)   E. Fragment

8. Cold-blooded animals such as snakes and other reptiles.
   E. Complete Sentence   (H. Fragment)

9. Insects, fish, frogs, and other creatures.
   U. Complete Sentence   (P. Fragment)

H	i	P	P	o	P	o	T	a	m	u	s
8	3	9	9	6	9	6	1	5	4	7	2

© Gary Robert Muschla

1.16 Outlaw Hero

Long ago, Robin Hood was an outlaw hero in England. It was said that he robbed from the rich and gave to the poor. Where did Robin Hood and his men live?

To answer the question, read each sentence below. Decide if it is correct or if it is a run-on sentence. Write the letter of each answer in the space above its sentence number at the bottom of the page. You will need to divide the letters into words.

1. Robin Hood was an outlaw, he lived in England.
   U. Correct Sentence   W. Run-On

2. Some historians believe that Robin was a real person.
   F. Correct Sentence   O. Run-On

3. Others believe he was only a legend.
   H. Correct Sentence   O. Run-On

4. There are many stories of Robin Hood all are interesting.
   T. Correct Sentence   D. Run-On

5. Robin robbed the rich, and he gave money to the poor.
   T. Correct Sentence   S. Run-On

6. Robin had many friends, his best friend was Little John.
   N. Correct Sentence   E. Run-On

7. The sheriff of Nottingham sent men to capture Robin.
   S. Correct Sentence   L. Run-On

8. The men searched everywhere they could not find him.
   D. Correct Sentence   R. Run-On

9. Robin Hood is the most famous English outlaw of all time.
   O. Correct Sentence   N. Run-On

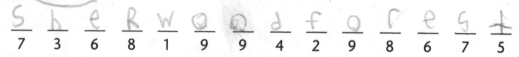

$$\frac{S}{7}\ \frac{h}{3}\ \frac{e}{6}\ \frac{R}{8}\ \frac{w}{1}\ \frac{o}{9}\ \frac{o}{9}\ \frac{d}{4}\ \frac{f}{2}\ \frac{o}{9}\ \frac{r}{8}\ \frac{e}{6}\ \frac{s}{7}\ \frac{t}{5}$$

© Gary Robert Muschla

1.17 Famous Woodpecker

Most people know of Woody Woodpecker, the famous cartoon character. But most people do not know he has a niece and a nephew. The name of Woody's niece is Knothead. What is the name of his nephew?

To answer the question, read each example below. Decide if it is a correct sentence, a run-on sentence, or a sentence fragment. Write the letter of each answer in the space above its number at the bottom of the page.

1. More than two hundred kinds of woodpeckers.
   E. Sentence   T. Run-On   (I. Fragment)

2. Woodpeckers are found in much of the world, they live in forests.
   V. Sentence   (E. Run-On)   Y. Fragment

3. Most woodpeckers eat insects.
   (P. Sentence)   A. Run-On   I. Fragment

4. They find insects by pecking at trees with their bills.
   (T. Sentence)   U. Run-On   H. Fragment

5. Ben Hardaway created Woody Woodpecker in 1940.
   (R. Sentence)   E. Run-On   J. Fragment

6. Woody's first film was *Knock Knock*, he soon became a cartoon star.
   J. Sentence   (N. Run-On)   L. Fragment

7. Starring in many cartoons over the years.
   P. Sentence   R. Run-On   (S. Fragment)

8. Children around the world know Woody they enjoy his cartoons.
   D. Sentence   (L. Run-On)   M. Fragment

$$\frac{S}{7} \quad \frac{P}{3} \quad \frac{L}{8} \quad \frac{i}{1} \quad \frac{n}{6} \quad \frac{T}{4} \quad \frac{e}{2} \quad \frac{r}{5}$$

© Gary Robert Muschla

1.18 Nickname for a President

Andrew Jackson was the seventh president of the United States. He had an unusual nickname. What was it?

To answer the question, name each of the examples below. Select your answers from the choices after each example. Write the letter of each answer in the space above its number at the bottom of the page. You will need to divide the letters into words.

1. When was Andrew Jackson born?
   N. Declarative Sentence   I. Interrogative Sentence   U. Fragment

2. Andrew Jackson was born on March 15, 1767, in South Carolina.
   R. Declarative Sentence   H. Run-On Sentence   N. Fragment

3. He became an orphan, he was raised by an uncle.
   D. Compound Sentence   K. Run-On Sentence   S. Fragment

4. Jackson was a man of great courage and a strong will.
   L. Declarative Sentence   R. Run-On Sentence   C. Fragment

5. Became a leader of the state of Tennessee.
   P. Interrogative Sentence   N. Run-On Sentence   Y. Fragment

6. Jackson fought in the War of 1812, and he was a hero.
   H. Compound Sentence   N. Run-On Sentence   L. Fragment

7. He was given a nickname for his toughness.
   B. Interrogative Sentence   D. Declarative Sentence   O. Run-On Sentence

8. Did Andrew Jackson win the election for president in 1828?
   U. Declarative Sentence   O. Interrogative Sentence   I. Compound Sentence

9. Was elected for a second term in 1832.
   T. Declarative Sentence   O. Exclamatory Sentence   C. Fragment

$\underline{O}$ $\underline{L}$ $\underline{d}$ $\underline{h}$ $\underline{I}$ $\underline{C}$ $\underline{K}$ $\underline{O}$ $\underline{r}$ $\underline{y}$
  8   4   7   6   1   9   3   8   2   5

© Gary Robert Muschla

1.19 First Phone Call

Alexander Graham Bell invented the telephone. He made the first telephone call to his assistant. What was the name of Bell's assistant?

To answer the question, read each example below. Decide if it is a correctly written sentence. If the example is a correct sentence, write the letter for *correct* in the space above its number at the bottom of the page. If it is not correct, write the letter for *incorrect*. You will need to divide the letters into words.

1. The telephone is one of the greatest inventions of all time, people make billions of calls each day.

   U. Correct   M. Incorrect

2. Alexander Graham Bell made the first telephone call in 1876.

   N. Correct   S. Incorrect

3. Greatly changed the lives of people all over the world.

   A. Correct   H. Incorrect

4. Soon telephones became common.

   W. Correct   T. Incorrect

5. In time, the whole country was linked by telephone.

   A. Correct   E. Incorrect

6. Today, using cell phones every day.

   N. Correct   S. Incorrect

7. Ana takes her cell phone everywhere.

   O. Correct   L. Incorrect

8. She uses her phone to call people she takes pictures with it.

   W. Correct   T. Incorrect

T	h	o	M	a	S	W	a	t	S	o	n
8	3	7	1	5	6	4	5	8	6	7	2

© Gary Robert Muschla

1.20 Famous Woman Dentist

In 1866, this woman graduated from dental school in the United States. She was the first woman to do this. Who was she?

To answer the question, read each sentence below. Name the underlined part. Choose your answers from the choices after each sentence. Write the letter of each answer in the space above its sentence number at the bottom of the page. You will need to divide the letters into words.

1. Clean, strong teeth are important to your health.
   G. Simple Subject   B. Complete Subject   T. Compound Subject

2. Teeth help you chew your food.
   U. Simple Subject   L. Compound Subject   A. Simple Predicate

3. Dentists care for people's teeth.
   M. Simple Predicate   S. Compound Predicate   C. Complete Predicate

4. Your dentist checks your teeth for cavities.
   S. Simple Predicate   K. Compound Predicate   M. Complete Predicate

5. Dentists fill cavities and clean your teeth.
   O. Compound Predicate   A. Complete Predicate   K. Simple Predicate

6. Carla and her brother brush their teeth at least twice each day.
   C. Complete Subject   H. Compound Subject   L. Simple Predicate

7. They also use dental floss to clean their teeth.
   C. Simple Subject   L. Simple Predicate   S. Complete Predicate

8. The children visit their dentist two times each year.
   U. Simple Subject   J. Compound Subject   B. Complete Subject

9. Their teeth are clean and healthy.
   Y. Simple Subject   R. Simple Predicate   I. Compound Subject

S	U	C	Y	h	O	B	U	S
7	2	3	9	6	5	1	8	4

© Gary Robert Muschla

1.21 Cool Creation

In 1874, Robert N. Green invented this wonderful treat. What did Green invent?

To answer the question, read each statement below. Decide if it is true or false. If a statement is true, write the letter for *true* in the space above the statement's number at the bottom of the page. If a statement is false, write the letter for *false*. You will need to divide the letters into words.

1. An interrogative sentence ends with an exclamation point.
   O. True   S. False

2. A complete sentence has a subject and a predicate.
   R. True   L. False

3. The complete subject of a sentence is the main word or words in the simple subject.
   H. True   M. False

4. A declarative sentence asks a question.
   C. True   I. False

5. A fragment is a very short complete sentence.
   R. True   O. False

6. A compound predicate is made of two or more simple predicates that have the same subject.
   E. True   N. False

7. A run-on sentence is correct if it ends with a period.
   P. True   D. False

8. An imperative sentence gives an order.
   A. True   E. False

9. The complete predicate tells what the subject of a sentence is or does.
   C. True   A. False

—— —— —— —— —— —— —— —— —— —— —— ——
 4   9   6   9   2   6   8   3   1   5   7   8

© Gary Robert Muschla

Nouns

Nouns are words that name a person, place, thing, or idea. There are many different kinds of nouns you should know.

The tip sheets and worksheets that follow will help you in your study of nouns. The first tip sheet and Worksheets 2.1 through 2.4 focus on identifying common and proper nouns. Two tip sheets and Worksheets 2.5 through 2.7 focus on plural and irregular plural nouns; a tip sheet and Worksheets 2.8 through 2.10 address possessive nouns; and Worksheets 2.11 through 2.14 offer a review of nouns.

Nouns

• •

A *noun* names a person, place, thing, or idea. There are many different kinds of nouns.

- *Common nouns* name any person, place, thing, or idea.

    Examples: boy, girl, school, town, river, puppy, mountain, freedom

- *Proper nouns* name a particular person, place, thing, or idea.

    Examples: James, Maria, the United States of America, North America, Rio Grande River, Washington Monument, Canada, Pacific Ocean

- *Singular nouns* name one person, place, thing, or idea.

    Examples: student, day, night, bird, town, church, valley, city, tomato

- *Plural nouns* name more than one person, place, thing, or idea.

    Examples: students, days, nights, birds, towns, churches, valleys, cities, tomatoes

- *Possessive nouns* show ownership. They can be singular or plural. They require an apostrophe.

    Examples: James's book, the dog's bed, the girls' softball team, the puppies' toys, the children's bikes

© Gary Robert Muschla

2.1 Frontier Hero

This man was an American frontiersman. He led settlers into Kentucky. Who was he?

To answer the question, find the noun in each set of words below. Write the letter of the noun in the space above its line number at the bottom of the page. You will need to divide the letters into words.

1. U. about   D. heavy   S. and   E. clouds

2. O. are   E. houses   L. but   N. his

3. D. bring   Y. snowy   N. song   E. where

4. Y. with   P. follow   R. the   L. country

5. O. animals   A. when   S. that   W. slowly

6. O. chilly   S. played   N. valley   V. hers

7. Y. their   A. rabbit   J. off   N. careful

8. B. rain   A. such   I. walked   D. under

9. A. take   E. until   I. ran   D. flowers

10. J. next   H. there   I. students   R. like

11. O. bridge   V. not   B. using   S. we

D   a   n   i   e   L   B   o   o   n   e
9   7   3   10   1   4   8   11   5   6   2

© Gary Robert Muschla

2.2 Snakes

Most snakes are harmless to people. But some are poisonous. The biggest poisonous snake can grow up to eighteen feet long. What is its name?

To answer the question, read each sentence below. Find a noun. Choose your answers from the underlined words. Write the letter that is below the noun in the space above its sentence number at the bottom of the page. You will need to divide the letters into words.

1. There are about 2,500 different kinds of snakes.
   E   U   R

2. They are found in most of the warmer parts of the world.
   S   A   I

3. Snakes belong to a group of animals known as reptiles.
   G   C   P

4. Most snakes have long, slender bodies.
   T   D   N

5. Some snakes are small and grow only inches.
   N   S   A

6. Other snakes may grow to be several feet long.
   O   L   I

7. Snakes may live on the ground, in water, or even on trees.
   T   G   U

8. Many snakes eat insects and small animals.
   M   K   T

9. Some people are frightened by snakes.
   E   B   C

K	i	n	g	C	o	b	r	a
8	2	4	7	3	6	9	1	5

© Gary Robert Muschla

Nouns

2.3 Surrounded States

These two states each touch eight other states. What states are they?

    To answer the question, read each sentence below. Find the underlined common or proper noun. Only one noun is underlined in each sentence. Write the letter of the noun in the space above its sentence number at the bottom of the page. You will need to divide the letters into words.

1. Traci is <u>doing</u> a <u>report</u> on <u>the</u> states.
            Y   Ⓞ   N

2. She <u>found</u> <u>much</u> information on the <u>Internet</u>.
          N   L   Ⓣ

3. California has the <u>most</u> <u>people</u> of <u>any</u> state.
             E   Ⓡ   H

4. Alaska is the <u>largest</u> state in the <u>country</u>.
           N   S Ⓜ

5. Swedish <u>settlers</u> <u>built</u> the <u>first</u> log cabins in Delaware.
          Ⓤ   H   T

6. <u>Mammoth Cave</u> in Kentucky is a <u>large</u> <u>underground</u> cave.
          Ⓘ   E   K

7. <u>Fewer</u> people live in Wyoming <u>than</u> in any other <u>state</u>.
   N   D   Ⓔ

8. Rainbow Bridge in Utah <u>is</u> a <u>natural</u> stone <u>bridge</u>.
          I   A   Ⓝ

9. Hawaii is <u>completely</u> <u>surrounded</u> by the <u>Pacific Ocean</u>.
          W   G   Ⓢ

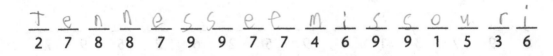

Tennessee missouri
2 7 8 8 7 9 9 7 7 4 6 9 9 1 5 3 6

© Gary Robert Muschla

Nouns

2.4 Going West

Many American settlers traveled west in this vehicle. What was it?

To answer the question, read each sentence below. Decide if the underlined word is a common or proper noun. Write the letter of each answer in the space above its sentence number at the bottom of the page. You will need to divide the letters into words.

1. <u>Settlers</u> went west to find new homes.
   S. Common   N. Proper

2. <u>St. Louis</u> was the starting point for many pioneers.
   K. Common   A. Proper

3. Their <u>journey</u> was long and dangerous.
   E. Common   M. Proper

4. They crossed rivers, plains, and <u>mountains</u>.
   T. Common   R. Proper

5. <u>People</u> might die of disease or a lack of food.
   G. Common   B. Proper

6. The <u>Rocky Mountains</u> must be crossed.
   U. Common   W. Proper

7. Many hoped to settle in <u>California</u>.
   P. Common   N. Proper

8. Others hoped to build homes in <u>Oregon</u> or Washington.
   U. Common   C. Proper

9. <u>Men</u>, women, and children traveled westward.
   O. Common   C. Proper

```
 C  O  N  E  N  T  O  G  A  W  A  G  O  N
 8  9  7  3  1  4  9  5  2  6  2  5  9  7
```

© Gary Robert Muschla

Nouns

Forming Plural Nouns

· ·

Follow the rules below to form plural nouns.

- For most nouns, add *-s*.

  Examples: student—students, tree—trees, river—rivers

- For nouns that end in *-s, -x, -ch, -sh,* or *-zz,* add *-es*.

  Examples: guess—guesses, box—boxes, church—churches, bush—bushes, buzz—buzzes

- For nouns that end with a vowel and *-y,* add *-s*.

  Examples: day—days, toy—toys, turkey—turkeys

- For nouns that end with a consonant and *-y,* change the *-y* to *-i* and add *-es*.

  Examples: country—countries, puppy—puppies

- For some nouns that end in *-f* or *-fe,* change the *-f* to *-v* and add *-s*. For some change the *-f* to *-v* and add *-es*. For some others, only add *-s*.

  Examples: wife—wives, calf—calves, chief—chiefs

- For nouns that end with a vowel and *-o,* add *-s*.

  Examples: radio—radios, video—videos

- For most nouns that end with a consonant and *-o,* add *-es*. For some, add *-s*.

  Examples: tomato—tomatoes, hero—heroes, silo—silos

© Gary Robert Muschla

· ·

2.5 Famous Signature

This man was the first to sign the Declaration of Independence. Who was he?

To answer the question, match each singular noun with its plural form. Write the letter of each answer in the space above its line number at the bottom of the page. You will need to divide the letters into words.

1. wife	I. wifes	N. wives
2. wish	A. wishs	O. wishes
3. lunch	H. lunches	U. lunchs
4. turkey	R. turkies	O. turkeys
5. horse	W. horsies	N. horses
6. berry	K. berries	T. berrys
7. radio	N. radioes	C. radios
8. tomato	H. tomatoes	M. tomatos
9. puppy	K. puppys	A. puppies
10. chief	J. chiefs	T. chieves
11. box	C. boxes	N. boxs

J	o	h	n	h	k	n	c	o	c	k
10	4	8	5	3	9	1	7	2	11	6

Nouns

© Gary Robert Muschla

2.6 Up, Up, and Away

The first hot-air balloon to carry people was invented by two French brothers. What was their last name?

To answer the question, complete each sentence below with the correct form of the plural noun. Choose your answers from the words after each sentence. Write the letter of each answer in the space above its sentence number at the bottom of the page. The first names of the brothers are given.

1. Amanda's uncle enjoys flying in hot-air _____.
   U. balloones   T. balloons

2. Uncle Charlie tells her _____ of his adventures.
   K. storys   F. stories

3. He tells her how he loves flying in clear _____.
   E. skies   U. skys

4. One time, he flew over four _____.
   N. counties   C. countys

5. Another time, he landed in thorny _____.
   G. bushes   M. bushs

6. Still another time, he landed in a tree's _____.
   O. branchs   I. branches

7. Once, he landed in the middle of a flock of wild _____.
   R. turkies   L. turkeys

8. Uncle Charlie visited Amanda's class and told the _____ about flying.
   R. studentes   M. students

9. He explained that manned balloon _____ began in 1783 in France.
   Ø. flights   I. flightes

10. To Uncle Charlie, those people were real _____.
    R. heroes   S. heros

Joseph and Jacques M O N T G O L F I e r
                    8 9 4 1 5 9 7 2 6 3 10

© Gary Robert Muschla

Nouns

Nouns with Special Plural Forms

The plural forms of most nouns are made by adding -s or -es. But some nouns are not made plural by adding -s or -es. These nouns have *irregular* plural forms. For some of these nouns, the singular and plural forms are spelled differently. For others, the singular and plural forms are the same.

The following are examples of nouns that have different singular and plural forms:

child—children	ox—oxen
foot—feet	man—men
mouse—mice	woman—women
goose—geese	tooth—teeth

The following are examples of nouns that have the same singular and plural forms:

sheep—sheep	series—series
moose—moose	traffic—traffic
deer—deer	salmon—salmon
trout—trout	wheat—wheat

© Gary Robert Muschla

2.7 Fast-Food First

Most Americans like hamburgers. The first fast-food hamburger company was started in 1921. This company is still serving hamburgers today. What is this company's name?

To answer the question, match each singular noun with its plural form. Write the letter of each answer in the space above its line number at the bottom of the page. You will need to divide the letters into words.

1. foot   N. foots   A. feet

2. deer   R. deers   T. deer

3. tooth   E. teeth   H. tooths

4. child   S. childes   E. children

5. mouse   T. mice   M. mouses

6. man   H. men   U. mans

7. sheep   D. sheeps   C. sheep

8. moose   I. moose   T. meese

9. goose   E. goose   L. geese

10. ox   W. oxen   B. oxes

11. woman   G. womans   S. women

W   h   i   T   e   C   a   s   T   L   e
10 6   8   2   3   7   1   11 5   9   4

© Gary Robert Muschla

Nouns

Possessive Nouns

A *possessive noun* shows ownership. It shows that a thing belongs to someone or something. Apostrophes are used to show the possessive case. Possessive nouns may be singular or plural.

- To write the possessive form of a singular noun, add an apostrophe and -s.

    Example: a cell phone that belongs to Cara—Cara's cell phone

    More examples: Joni's gloves, James's pen, the hamster's cage, New Jersey's beaches

- To write the possessive form of a plural noun that ends in -s, add an apostrophe after the -s.

    Example: the bikes of the students—the students' bikes

    More examples: the puppies' bed, the boys' basketball team, the Smiths' boat

- To write the possessive form of a plural noun that does not end in -s, add an apostrophe and -s.

    Example: the coats of the children—the children's coats

    More examples: the women's ski team, the mice's nest, the oxen's plow

© Gary Robert Muschla

2.8 Famous Crime Fighter

Most Batman fans know that Bruce Wayne is Batman. What were the names of Bruce Wayne's parents?

To answer the question, match each singular noun with its called for singular possessive or plural possessive form. Write the letter of each answer in the space above its line number at the bottom of the page. You will need to divide the letters into words.

1. policeman (singular possessive)   K. policemans'   ⬭S. policeman's

2. street (singular possessive)   R. street's   I. streets'

3. butler (singular possessive)   U. butlers'   ⬭H. butler's

4. city (plural possessive)   ⬭U. city's   O. cities'

5. Robin (singular possessive)   L. Robins'   M. Robin's

6. child (plural possessive)   I. childs'   ⬭A. children's

7. crook (plural possessive)   ⬭A. crooks'   E. crook's

8. citizen (singular possessive)   ⬭H. citizen's   R. citizens'

9. hero (plural possessive)   ⬭T. heroes'   P. hero's

10. Bruce (singular possessive)   ⬭T. Bruce's   L. Bruces'

11. girl (plural possessive)   ⬭A. girls'   N. girl's

12. man (plural possessive)   I. mans'   ⬭M. men's

T	h	o	m	a	s	m	a	r	T	h	a
10	8	4	12	6	1	5	11	2	9	3	7

© Gary Robert Muschla

Nouns

2.9 Guide to Freedom

This former slave helped guide other slaves to freedom. She was called the "Moses of her people." Who was she?

To answer the question, find the correct possessive noun in each pair of words below. The correct noun may be singular or plural. Write the letter of each answer in the space above its number at the bottom of the page. You will need to divide the letters into words.

1. S. countrys'   N. leader's

2. I. friends'   T. puppys'

3. S. womans'   U. painter's

4. E. kittens'   N. babys'

5. M. aunt's   A. citys'

6. P. deers'   H. teachers'

7. B. storm's   C. cars's

8. R. schools'   V. doctors's

9. O. wifes'   T. flower's

10. R. mices'   A. horses'

H a r r i e T r u b M a n
6 10 8 8 2 4 9 9 3 7 5 10 1

© Gary Robert Muschla

Nouns

2.10 Famous Monument

Presidents George Washington, Thomas Jefferson, Abraham Lincoln, and Theodore Roosevelt are shown in this famous memorial. What is the name of this memorial?

To answer the question, read each sentence below. Find the singular or plural possessive noun. Decide if the possessive noun is used correctly. If it is correct, write the letter for *correct* in the space above its sentence number at the bottom of the page. If it is incorrect, write the letter for *incorrect*. You will need to divide the letters into words.

1. Jessica's class is learning about the presidents.
   S. Correct   I. Incorrect

2. Each students' assignment includes a report.
   G. Correct   E. Incorrect

3. Armando's report was about George Washington.
   T. Correct   N. Incorrect

4. Washington's leadership helped win the Revolutionary War.
   H. Correct   D. Incorrect

5. He was our country's first president.
   N. Correct   S. Incorrect

6. Thomas Jefferson helped write our young nations' laws.
   A. Correct   O. Incorrect

7. Abraham Lincolns' Gettysburg Address was a great speech.
   M. Correct   U. Incorrect

8. Theodore Roosevelt was one of Americas' youngest presidents.
   C. Correct   M. Incorrect

9. Mrs. Harris, the schools' principal, praised the students for their good work.
   J. Correct   R. Incorrect

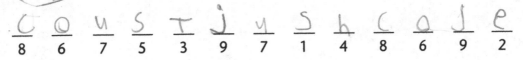

C	O	u	S	T	j	u	S	h	C	O	J	e
8	6	7	5	3	9	7	1	4	8	6	9	2

© Gary Robert Muschla

Nouns

2.11 Pluto

The astronomer Clyde William Tombaugh discovered Pluto in 1930. But several years earlier, another astronomer predicted that Pluto would one day be found. Who was this astronomer?

To answer the question, read the article below. Decide if the underlined words are nouns. Not all of the nouns in the article are underlined. Start with the first sentence. Then write the letters beneath the underlined nouns in order in the spaces at the bottom of the page.

Pluto is a dwarf planet in our solar system. Some astronomers believe that Pluto
P   H   E   A   R   S

was once a moon of Neptune. Neptune is the eighth planet from the sun. Pluto is
C   I   W

named after the Roman god of the underworld. Pluto is small, cold, and lifeless. It
V   A   J   T   K

can only be seen through powerful telescopes. Astronomers think that Pluto's
S   L   R

surface is made of frozen gases, ice, and rock. It will be a long time before any
L   P   O   W   E   M   L

humans visit this far-off world.
L   S

P e r c i v a l   L o w e l l

© Gary Robert Muschla

Nouns

2.12 Sources of Energy

Most of the energy produced in the United States comes from these sources. What are these sources of energy?

To answer the question, match the noun on the left with its most accurate label on the right. Write the letter of each answer in the space above the noun's number at the bottom of the page.

Noun

1. students'
2. teeth
3. Rosa
4. Americans
5. town
6. father's
7. cities
8. flowers
9. potatoes
10. Justin's
11. bird

Label

L. singular, common
S. plural, common
U. singular, proper
I. plural, proper
O. plural, irregular
F. singular possessive
E. plural possessive

$\underline{U}$ $\underline{F}$ $\underline{L}$ $\underline{F}$ $\underline{U}$ $\underline{S}$ $\quad$ $\underline{L}$ $\underline{O}$ $\underline{S}$ $\underline{S}$ $\underline{O}$
10 2   7   9   4   5   6   3   1   11 8

© Gary Robert Muschla

2.13 Snowy City

Except for places in Alaska, this city in New York is the snowiest in the United States. It receives about 110 inches of snow each year. What city is this?

To answer the question, complete each sentence below with the correct form of the noun. Choose your answers from the words after each sentence. Write the letter of each answer in the space above its sentence number at the bottom of the page.

1. A big snowstorm hit _____ town yesterday.
   C. Jennifer's   M. Jennifers'

2. _____ throughout the area were closed.
   L. Schooles   S. Schools

3. Two _____ of snow fell overnight.
   E. foots   R. feet

4. Jennifer and her sister Rachel built three _____.
   S. snowmans   E. snowmen

5. Rachel and some _____ built a snowfort.
   A. friends   R. friendes

6. All of the _____ had an exciting snowball fight.
   E. childrens   U. children

7. Rachel's team declared themselves the _____.
   S. winners   B. winner's

8. It turned out to be one of the best _____ of the year.
   Y. days   I. dayes

$$\underline{B} \quad \underline{Y} \quad \underline{r} \quad \underline{a} \quad \underline{C} \quad \underline{u} \quad \underline{S} \quad \underline{e}$$
$$7 \quad\quad 8 \quad\quad 3 \quad\quad 5 \quad\quad 1 \quad\quad 6 \quad\quad 2 \quad\quad 4$$

© Gary Robert Muschla

2.14 Game for Kids

Eleanor Abbott invented this popular game for children. What is the name of the game?

To answer the question, read each statement below. Decide if it is true or false. If the statement is true, write the letter for *true* in the space above its number at the bottom of the page. If the statement is false, write the letter for *false*. You will need to divide the letters into words.

1. A noun names a person, place, or thing, but not an idea.
   O. True   N. False

2. Nouns may be singular or plural.
   N. True   O. False

3. Some nouns have the same form in both the singular and the plural.
   A. True   E. False

4. Not all proper nouns must be capitalized.
   U. True   A. False

5. Plural nouns always end in *-s* or *-es*.
   L. True   Y. False

6. Possessive nouns show ownership.
   D. True   H. False

7. Common nouns can never be plural.
   T. True   C. False

8. Possessive nouns must have an apostrophe.
   D. True   E. False

9. Proper nouns only refer to people.
   T. True   L. False

C e Q e Y L v n D
7 3 1 8 5 9 4 2 6

© Gary Robert Muschla

Verbs

Verbs are words that express action or state of being. Along with a subject, every sentence must have a verb.

The following tip sheets and worksheets focus on verbs and verb usage. The first tip sheet and Worksheets 3.1 through 3.10 cover action verbs, verb phrases, and linking verbs. Another tip sheet and Worksheets 3.11 and 3.12 focus on direct objects. One tip sheet and Worksheet 3.13 concentrate on nouns (predicate nominatives) and adjectives (predicate adjectives) that follow linking verbs. A tip sheet and Worksheet 3.14 concentrate on verb contractions with *not*. Two tip sheets and Worksheets 3.15 through 3.17 cover verb tenses. One tip sheet and Worksheets 3.18 through 3.20 cover subject and verb agreement. One tip sheet and Worksheets 3.21 through 3.23 address irregular verbs, and one tip sheet and Worksheets 3.24 and 3.25 provide added material for the verbs *be* and *have*. Finally, Worksheets 3.26 through 3.29 provide reviews of verbs.

Two Kinds of Verbs

There are two kinds of verbs in English: action and linking.

- An *action verb* tells what the subject of a sentence does or did.

  Anthony <u>plays</u> the drums in the school band.

  Elena <u>watched</u> a scary movie last night.

  The deer <u>ran</u> across the field.

- A *linking verb* links, or connects, the subject of a sentence with a noun or adjective in the predicate. A word that follows a linking verb names or describes the subject. Forms of the verb *be—am, is, are, was, were, being,* and *been—*are linking verbs.

  Lindsay <u>was</u> happy.

  Joe <u>is</u> a great soccer player.

  I <u>am</u> thirsty.

- Other verbs such as *appear, become, feel, grow, sound, seem, look,* and *taste* can also be linking verbs. To be linking verbs, these verbs must be able to take the place of a form of the verb *be* in a sentence.

  Megan <u>seemed</u> shocked.

  Megan <u>was</u> shocked.

  The kittens <u>look</u> sleepy.

  The kittens <u>are</u> sleepy.

- A verb that contains more than one word is called a *verb phrase*. The last word in the phrase is the *main verb*. All other words in the phrase are *helping verbs*. There are many helping verbs. Here are some of the most common: *am, are, is, was, were, be, have, has, had, do, does, did, will, would, shall, should, can, could, may, might.*

  Kim <u>is studying</u> for her math test.

  Bryan <u>has finished</u> his science report.

  We <u>will be going</u> to Europe this summer.

© Gary Robert Muschla

3.1 Author of a Classic Story

P. L. Travers wrote *Mary Poppins*. What do the initials *P. L.* stand for?

To answer the question, find the action verb in each set of words below. Write the letter of the action verb in the space above its line number at the bottom of the page. The first letter of the author's name is given.

1. O. happy	N. walked	H. large	Y. from
2. C. quick	N. chilly	I. you	E. swam
3. K. below	O. do	D. sadly	R. fast
4. O. they	E. any	A. write	I. book
5. M. month	T. pretty	B. careful	Y. ran
6. A. sun	M. finished	C. hot	E. rain
7. N. sing	E. onto	S. bee	Y. day
8. I. spider	U. cloudy	L. cried	A. after
9. L. studied	M. planet	C. ocean	T. father
10. E. we	N. year	M. scary	A. hiked
11. W. turtle	R. street	D. see	I. pond

P a m e L a   L Y n d O n
__ __ __ __ __ __   __ __ __ __ __ __
   10 6 2 8 4   9 5 1 11 3 7

© Gary Robert Muschla

Verbs

49

3.2 Flying While Sleeping

This big seabird can sleep while flying over the ocean. What kind of bird is this?

To answer the question, read each sentence below. Find the action verb. Choose your answers from the underlined words. Write the letter beneath the verb in the space above its sentence number at the bottom of the page.

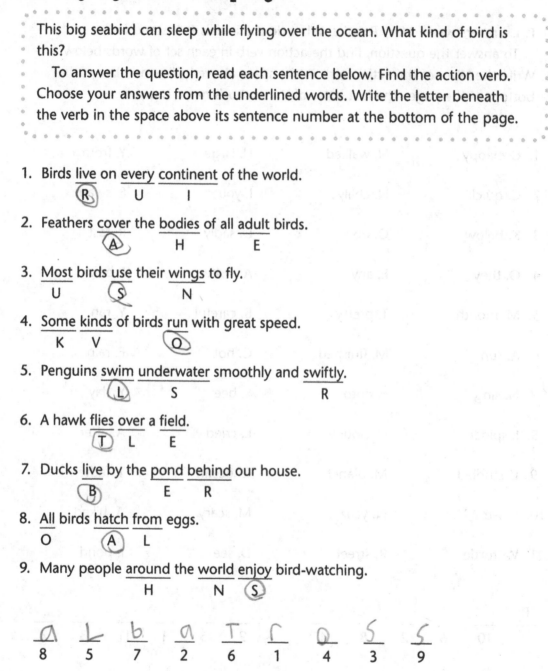

1. Birds live on every continent of the world.
   (R)   U   I

2. Feathers cover the bodies of all adult birds.
   (A)   H   E

3. Most birds use their wings to fly.
   U   (S)   N

4. Some kinds of birds run with great speed.
   K   V   (O)

5. Penguins swim underwater smoothly and swiftly.
   (L)   S   R

6. A hawk flies over a field.
   (T)   L   E

7. Ducks live by the pond behind our house.
   (B)   E   R

8. All birds hatch from eggs.
   O   (A)   L

9. Many people around the world enjoy bird-watching.
   H   N   (S)

   A   L   b   a   T   r   o   S   S
   8   5   7   2   6   1   4   3   9

Verbs

© Gary Robert Muschla

3.3 A Philadelphia First

In 1752, Philadelphia was the first city in the thirteen colonies to have one of these. What was this "first"?

To answer the question, read each sentence below. Find the action verb. Choose your answers from the underlined words. Write the letter beneath the verb in the space above its sentence number at the bottom of the page.

1. Swedish settlers came to this area in the 1640s.
   K   (T)   H

2. William Penn planned a city in the early 1680s.
        (O)   U   E

3. He named his new city Philadelphia.
      (I)   E   R

4. Penn founded a colony with religious freedom.
      (L)   N   S

5. Soon many immigrants from Europe arrived.
        N   T   (S)

6. The small city grew rapidly in population and importance.
      H   (P)   T

7. Ben Franklin moved to Philadelphia in 1729.
       (H)   L   C

8. Philadelphia played a major role in the Revolutionary War.
      (A)   E   N

h   a   s   p   i   t   a   l
7   2   5   6   3   1   8   4

© Gary Robert Muschla

Verbs

3.4 Planets and Stars

The word *planet* comes from the ancient Greeks. What did the Greeks call a planet?

To answer the question, read each sentence below. Find the verb phrase. In the parentheses after each sentence, a letter is called for. Find this letter in the verb phrase. Write the letter in the space above the verb phrase's sentence number at the bottom of the page. The first one is done for you.

1. A clear night <u>is filled</u> with stars. (eighth letter)

2. People have studied the night sky for thousands of years. (ninth letter)

3. The ancient Greeks were puzzled by the stars and planets. (second letter)

4. Ancient astronomers would imagine pictures in the night sky. (ninth letter)

5. Most people can see these pictures today. (fourth letter)

6. These pictures are known as constellations. (seventh letter)

7. You may have trouble finding planets. (fifth letter)

8. People might confuse planets with stars. (eighth letter)

9. Unlike a planet, a star will twinkle. (fifth letter)

10. Planets will travel slowly across the night sky on their own paths. (sixth letter)

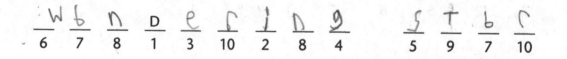

W	b	n	D	e	r	i	n	g		S	t	b	r
6	7	8	1	3	10	2	8	4		5	9	7	10

Verbs

© Gary Robert Muschla

3.5 Aiming for the Stars

On October 4, 1957, the Soviet Union sent the first satellite into space. What was the name of this satellite?

To answer the question, read the article below. Decide if the underlined words are verb phrases. Start with the first sentence. Then write the letters beneath the verb phrases in order in the spaces at the bottom of the page.

For thousands of years, people <u>have dreamed</u> of exploring space. But spaceflight
S

<u>was impossible</u>. This <u>finally changed</u> in 1957. That year the first satellite <u>was sent</u> into
E   X   P

space. The satellite <u>stayed in</u> space for twenty-one days. This satellite <u>was followed</u> by
R   U

others. Both the Soviet Union and the United States <u>launched many</u> satellites. By the
V

mid-1960s, scientists <u>had learned</u> much about space. Many humans <u>had flown</u> in space.
T   N

The United States <u>hoped to</u> land astronauts on the moon. This <u>would be</u> a great
O   I

achievement. Finally, on July 20, 1969, American astronauts <u>landed on</u> the moon.
R

Travel to another world <u>had been achieved</u>. Space <u>was now</u> the new frontier.
K   S

_S_ _P_ _R_ _U_ _T_ _N_ _O_

© Gary Robert Muschla

Verbs

3.6 Nighttime Animals

Most animals are active during the daylight hours. But some are active at night. What are these "night" animals called?

To answer the question, read each sentence below. Decide if the underlined verb is a linking verb. If the verb is a linking verb, write the letter for *yes* in the space above its sentence number at the bottom of the page. If the verb is not a linking verb, write the letter for *no*.

1. Many animals <u>are</u> more active at night than during the day.
   U. Yes   H. No

2. These animals <u>sleep</u> during the day.
   A. Yes   O. No

3. Owls <u>hunt</u> during the night.
   R. Yes   L. No

4. Owls <u>have</u> excellent eyesight for seeing in the dark.
   E. Yes   A. No

5. An aardvark <u>is</u> a large animal.
   R. Yes   S. No

6. Aardvarks <u>eat</u> ants and other insects during the night.
   T. Yes   C. No

7. Last night Lisa and her brother <u>were</u> outside.
   N. Yes   S. No

8. They <u>saw</u> a bat chasing moths.
   H. Yes   T. No

9. The bat <u>was</u> a swift flier.
   N. Yes   M. No

```
 N   O   C   t   u   r   n   e   L
 7   2   6   8   1   5   9   4   3
```

© Gary Robert Muschla

Verbs

3.7 Not an Ordinary Tornado

Tornadoes do not always occur on land. Sometimes a tornado forms over water. What is this kind of tornado called?

To answer the question, read each sentence below. Find the linking verb. Choose your answers from the underlined words. Write the letter beneath each linking verb in the space above its sentence number at the bottom of the page.

1. A tornado is a very powerful storm.
    (E)   H   F

2. Tornadoes are violent storms of whirling winds.
        (O)   D   U

3. Even from far away, tornadoes appear terrifying.
        I   (A)   U

4. My grandfather was a weather forecaster.
    E   (R)   A

5. He and his staff were experts on tornadoes.
        O   F   (A)

6. I am curious about tornadoes.
    (S)   L   E

7. To me the power of a tornado seems unstoppable.
    (L)   B   P

8. They are extremely destructive storms.
        (W)   R   C

9. No one is safe near a tornado.
        F (T)   E

W a T e r S L o a T
8 5 9 1 4 6 7 2 3 9

© Gary Robert Muschla

Verbs

55

3.8 Related to Mickey

Mickey Mouse, the famous cartoon character, has two nephews. What are their names?

To answer the question, find the called for action or linking verb in each set of words below. Write the letter of the verb in the space above its line number at the bottom of the page. You will need to divide the letters into words.

1. Action	U. favorite	E. cheered	I. be
2. Linking	V. either	L. pretty	O. were
3. Action	T. throw	B. to	H. under
4. Action	R. hero	J. sunny	A. send
5. Linking	L. wonderful	F. am	T. talk
6. Action	A. from	M. caught	U. been
7. Linking	S. walked	N. is	R. or
8. Action	D. slipped	R. careless	S. one
9. Linking	U. her	O. called	R. was
10. Linking	Y. are	J. excited	I. beautiful

M O R T Y A n d F e R D y
6 2 9 3 10 4 7 8 5 1 9 8 10

56

© Gary Robert Muschla

3.9 Busy Bees

Bees make honey from the nectar of flowers. To make a pound of honey, bees must collect nectar from a lot of flowers. About how many flowers must bees visit to collect enough nectar to make one pound of honey?

To answer the question, read each sentence below. Decide if the underlined verb is an action verb or a linking verb. If it is an action verb, write the letter for *action* in the space above its sentence number at the bottom of the page. If it is a linking verb, write the letter for *linking*. You will need to divide the letters into words.

1. Honeybees are busy insects.
   S. Action   W. Linking

2. Honeybees gather the nectar of flowers to make honey.
   O. Action   G. Linking

3. Bees use honey for food.
   N. Action   E. Linking

4. Bears and other animals eat honey.
   T. Action   N. Linking

5. Most kinds of honey taste sweet.
   I. Action   L. Linking

6. The queen bee is the most important bee in the hive.
   T. Action   I. Linking

7. Worker bees collect nectar and pollen.
   I. Action   S. Linking

8. A beehive becomes home to thousands of bees.
   L. Action   M. Linking

9. Roberto found a beehive in his backyard.
   L. Action   C. Linking

10. He was careful not to disturb the hive.
    E. Action   O. Linking

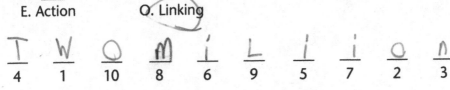

T	W	O	M	i	L	i	i	O	n
4	1	10	8	6	9	5	7	2	3

© Gary Robert Muschla

Verbs

3.10 Hurricanes by Another Name

Hurricanes are powerful storms that form in the Atlantic Ocean. What are the powerful storms that form in the Pacific Ocean called?

To answer the question, read each sentence below. Find the verb. Decide if the verb is an action verb or a linking verb. If it is an action verb, write the letter for *action* in the space above its sentence number at the bottom of the page. If it is a linking verb, write the letter for *linking*.

1. Hurricanes are mighty ocean storms.
   N. Action   H. Linking

2. Upon reaching land, they cause great destruction.
   N. Action   S. Linking

3. The winds of a powerful hurricane reach two hundred miles per hour.
   O. Action   M. Linking

4. My grandmother owns a house near the coast.
   S. Action   I. Linking

5. She is afraid of hurricanes.
   S. Action   Y. Linking

6. Last summer a storm became a hurricane.
   N. Action   O. Linking

7. My grandmother was ready to travel inland to safety.
   H. Action   T. Linking

8. Fortunately, the hurricane did not come near land.
   P. Action   E. Linking

$$\underset{7}{T} \quad \underset{5}{Y} \quad \underset{8}{p} \quad \underset{1}{h} \quad \underset{3}{o} \quad \underset{6}{n} \quad \underset{2}{n} \quad \underset{4}{i}$$

Verbs

© Gary Robert Muschla

Direct Objects

In some sentences an action verb is followed by a noun or pronoun. This noun or pronoun is called a *direct object*. Here are some facts and examples of direct objects:

- A direct object is a noun or pronoun in the predicate of a sentence.

- A direct object follows an action verb and receives the action of the verb. (Direct objects do not follow linking verbs.)

- A direct object answers the question *whom?* or *what?*

- A sentence may have one, two, or more direct objects.

   Miguel found the <u>book</u>. (What did Miguel find? *book*)

   Hannah called <u>me</u>. (Whom did Hannah call? *me*)

   Catalina plays the <u>violin</u> and <u>piano</u>. (What does Catalina play? *violin* and *piano*)

© Gary Robert Muschla

3.11 What's the Weather?

When we want to know what the weather is going to be, we watch or listen to a weather forecast. What is a person who studies and reports the weather called?

To answer the question, read each sentence below. Decide if the underlined word is a direct object. If the word is a direct object, write the letter for *yes* in the space above its sentence number at the bottom of the page. If the word is not a direct object, write the letter for *no*.

1. Beth's father builds <u>houses</u> for a living.
   (I. Yes)   A. No

2. He listens to the weather report <u>every</u> morning.
   N. Yes   (L. No)

3. He wears light <u>clothing</u> in hot weather.
   R. Yes   (J. No)

4. He takes his <u>raincoat</u> for stormy weather.
   (E. Yes)   L. No

5. Beth is <u>interested</u> in the weather too.
   E. Yes   (S. No)

6. She was <u>caught</u> in the rain yesterday.
   (E. Yes)   G. No

7. Beth likes to swim on <u>sunny</u> summer days.
   (S. Yes)   M. No

8. Beth's brother enjoys the <u>winter</u>.
   (T. Yes)   I. No

9. He plays <u>hockey</u> in a junior league.
   (O. Yes)   W. No

$\underline{S}$ $\underline{e}$ $\underline{T}$ $\underline{e}$ $\underline{o}$ $\underline{J}$ $\underline{o}$ $\underline{L}$ $\underline{o}$ $\underline{e}$ $\underline{i}$ $\underline{S}$ $\underline{T}$
7   4   8   4   9   3   9   2   9   6   1   5   8

© Gary Robert Muschla

3.12 Walking on a Tightrope

Tightrope walkers perform in circuses and carnivals. What is a person who walks a tightrope called?

To answer the question, read each sentence below. Find the direct object. In the parentheses after each sentence, a letter is called for. Find this letter in the direct object. Write the letter in the space above the direct object's sentence number at the bottom of the page. The first one is done for you.

1. Jenna's Uncle Jimmy entertains <u>people</u>. (fifth letter)

2. Jenna watched her uncle's show at the circus. (first letter)

3. Uncle Jimmy crossed a wire high above the ground. (second letter)

4. Jenna clapped her hands in appreciation of his skill. (third letter)

5. The audience enjoyed the performance. (fourth letter)

6. Uncle Jimmy heard the applause. (first letter)

7. Someone threw a bouquet of flowers to him. (first letter)

8. He flashed a smile to the crowd. (second letter)

9. Each day he practices his act. (third letter)

10. He loves the circus. (fifth letter)

$$\frac{f}{5} \quad \frac{u}{10} \quad \frac{n}{4} \quad \frac{a}{6} \quad \frac{m}{8} \quad \frac{b}{7} \quad \frac{u}{10} \quad \frac{L}{1} \quad \frac{i}{3} \quad \frac{y}{2} \quad \frac{t}{9}$$

© Gary Robert Muschla

Verbs

Nouns and Adjectives That Follow Linking Verbs

Linking verbs do not show action. They link the subject of a sentence to a word in the predicate. This word may be a noun or adjective. Here are some facts and examples:

- A noun that follows a linking verb renames the subject of the sentence.

  Danny is a student. (*Student* renames *Danny.*)

  Mr. Simon was a teacher. (*Teacher* renames *Mr. Simon.*)

  Brian and Ashley are cousins. (*Cousins* renames *Brian* and *Ashley.*)

- An adjective that follows a linking verb describes the subject.

  The storm was powerful. (*Powerful* describes the *storm.*)

  The kitten was cute. (*Cute* describes *kitten.*)

  The puppies were afraid of the thunderstorm. (*Afraid* describes *puppies.*)

- Linking verbs may be followed by two or more words that rename or describe the subject.

  Mr. Simon was a teacher and a pilot.

  The kitten was cute and cuddly.

© Gary Robert Muschla

3.13 Favorite Cookie

According to the "experts," this is the most popular cookie. What is it?

To answer the question, read each sentence below. Decide if the underlined word renames or describes the subject of the sentence. If it does, write the letter for *yes* in the space above the word's sentence number at the bottom of the page. If the word does not rename or describe the subject, write the letter for *no*. You will need to divide the letters into words.

1. Yesterday I was working at a <u>bakery</u>.
   A. Yes   E. No

2. The bakery's owner is my <u>uncle</u>.
   A. Yes   S. No

3. He is an <u>expert</u> on cookies.
   I. Yes   O. No

4. His shop is filled with <u>cookies</u>.
   E. Yes   L. No

5. He became a <u>baker</u> many years ago.
   T. Yes   A. No

6. His cookies taste <u>great</u>.
   P. Yes   N. No

7. They are the <u>best</u> in the world.
   T. Yes   O. No

8. The cookies are very <u>tasty</u>.
   H. Yes   A. No

9. I am his <u>biggest</u> customer.
   I. Yes   C. No

j h o J o e s a e i n i e
9 8 7 9 7 4 2 5 1 9 8 3 6

© Gary Robert Muschla

Verbs

Contractions with *Not*

• •

A *contraction* is a short form of two words. An apostrophe is used to show that a letter or letters have been left out. Here are some facts and examples about contractions:

- Many contractions are made with verbs and the word *not*.

is not—isn't	was not—wasn't	are not—aren't
were not—weren't	do not—don't	did not—didn't
cannot—can't	could not—couldn't	has not—hasn't
had not—hadn't	have not—haven't	would not—wouldn't

- A special contraction is *won't*, which is made from *will not*.

© Gary Robert Muschla

3.14 Naming America

The name *America* comes from the name of an Italian explorer. This man explored the coast of the New World shortly after Columbus. Who was he?

To answer the question, match each pair of words on the left with the contraction they make on the right. Write the letter of each answer in the space above the number of each pair at the bottom of the page.

Words	Contractions
1. have not	O. aren't
2. do not	U. can't
3. were not	A. isn't
4. did not	C. won't
5. are not	S. don't
6. had not	I. couldn't
7. is not	G. wouldn't
8. cannot	E. hasn't
9. could not	R. haven't
10. has not	P. hadn't
11. will not	V. weren't
12. would not	M. didn't

A M E R I G O   V E S P U C C I
7 4 10 1 9 12 5   3 10 2 6 8 11 11 9

© Gary Robert Muschla

Verbs

Verb Tenses

The tense of a verb shows time. Tense shows when something in a sentence happens, happened, or will happen. The three main tenses of verbs follow.

- The *present tense* shows action that is happening now.

  Christy and her brother <u>walk</u> their dog.

- The *past tense* shows action that has happened.

  They <u>walked</u> their dog yesterday.

- The *future tense* shows action that will happen. It is formed by adding the helping verbs *will* or *shall* to the present-tense form of the verb.

  They <u>will walk</u> their dog tonight.

© Gary Robert Muschla

Rules for Forming the Tenses of Verbs

. . . .

The forms of most verbs change when their tense changes.

Present Tense

Follow these rules when the subject is a singular noun.

- To form the present tense of many verbs, add -s.
  talk—talks   call—calls   climb—climbs

- To form the present tense of verbs ending in -s, -ch, -sh, -x, and -z, add -es.
  guess—guesses   catch—catches   push—pushes
  fix—fixes   buzz—buzzes

- To form the present tense of verbs ending in a consonant and -y, change the -y
  to -i and add -es.
  try—tries   hurry—hurries   carry—carries

Past Tense

- To form the past tense of most verbs, add -ed. For verbs ending with -e, add -d.
  walk—walked   jump—jumped   hike—hiked

- To form the past tense of verbs ending with a consonant and -y, change the -y
  to -i and add -ed.
  try—tried   hurry—hurried   carry—carried

- To form the past tense of verbs ending with a single vowel and a consonant,
  double the final consonant and add -ed.
  ' stop—stopped   slip—slipped   wrap—wrapped

© Gary Robert Muschla

. . . .

3.15 Earthquakes

An earthquake is a violent shaking of the earth. Most earthquakes are caused by the movement of rocks far underground. What is a person who studies earthquakes called?

To answer the question, read each sentence below. Decide if the underlined verb is in the past, the present, or the future tense. Write the letter of each answer in the space above its sentence number at the bottom of the page.

1. Danielle will learn about earthquakes in science.
    R. Past   K. Present   M. Future

2. She enjoys learning about the earth.
    A. Past   E. Present   H. Future

3. She lives in California.
    V. Past   L. Present   D. Future

4. Two years ago an earthquake occurred in her area.
    T. Past   N. Present   L. Future

5. Fortunately, it caused only a little damage.
    G. Past   L. Present   N. Future

6. Danielle plans to be a scientist someday.
    L. Past   I. Present   J. Future

7. She will go to college to study earthquakes.
    Y. Past   S. Present   O. Future

8. She hopes to learn more about earthquakes.
    O. Past   S. Present   E. Future

S   e   i   s   m   o   L   o   G   i   s   t
8   2   6   8   1   7   3   7   5   6   8   4

© Gary Robert Muschla

Verbs

68

3.16 Food for Plants

Plants use sunlight and water and minerals from the soil to make food. What is this process called?

To answer the question, read each sentence below. Find the verb. Decide if the verb is in the past, the present, or the future tense. Write the letter of each answer in the space above its sentence number at the bottom of the page.

1. Most plants make their own food.
   A. Past   E. Present   J. Future

2. They need the energy of sunlight.
   I. Past   Y. Present   R. Future

3. Our class studied plants last week.
   N. Past   C. Present   T. Future

4. We grew bean plants in class.
   I. Past   Y. Present   T. Future

5. Next we will study animals in science.
   U. Past   I. Present   T. Future

6. I like learning about things in nature.
   T. Past   O. Present   K. Future

7. Maybe someday I will be a scientist.
   E. Past   A. Present   P. Future

8. My brother wanted to be a scientist, too.
   H. Past   O. Present   I. Future

9. Now he plans to become a doctor.
   N. Past   S. Present   L. Future

P h o t o s y n t h e s i s
7 8 6 5 6 9 2 3 5 8 1 9 4 9

© Gary Robert Muschla

Verbs

3.17 Coral Reef

The biggest coral reef in the world is found off the coast of Australia. It is about 1,250 miles long. What is the name of this reef?

To answer the question, read each sentence below. Decide if the verb tense is correct. If the tense is correct, write the letter for *correct* in the space above the sentence number at the bottom of the page. If the tense is incorrect, write the letter for *incorrect*. You will need to divide the letters into words.

1. Next summer Hallie and her family planned to go on vacation.
   L. Correct   H. Incorrect

2. They will go to Australia in July.
   B. Correct   N. Incorrect

3. Yesterday Hallie's mother will meet with a travel agent.
   T. Correct   I. Incorrect

4. Hallie hopes to see kangaroos in Australia.
   A. Correct   O. Incorrect

5. The flight to Australia from California will be long.
   G. Correct   R. Incorrect

6. Last year the family visits the Grand Canyon.
   B. Correct   T. Incorrect

7. They traveled to the Grand Canyon by car.
   E. Correct   U. Incorrect

8. Hallie enjoyed the upcoming trip to Australia.
   N. Correct   R. Incorrect

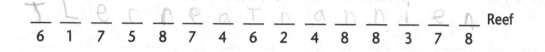

T L e r r e a T n a n n i e n Reef
6 1 7 5 8 7 4 6 2 4 8 8 3 7 8

Verbs

© Gary Robert Muschla

Agreement Between Subjects and Verbs

Subjects must agree with their verbs in number. A singular subject needs the singular form of a verb. A plural subject needs the plural form of a verb.

- In the present tense, add -s or -es to the verb when the subject is singular. Do not add -s or -es when the subject is plural.

  Sean <u>plays</u> soccer on the middle school team. (singular, present tense)

  The brothers <u>play</u> soccer on the middle school team. (plural, present tense)

  Sean <u>goes</u> to practice after school. (singular, present tense)

  The brothers <u>go</u> to practice after school. (plural, present tense)

- In the present tense, the pronouns *I* and *you* need the plural forms of verbs. Do not add -s or -es to the verbs.

  I <u>walk</u> to school each day.

  You <u>walk</u> to school each day.

  The brothers <u>walk</u> to school each day.

- In the past tense, the singular and plural forms of most verbs end in -ed.

  Sean <u>played</u> soccer on the middle school team. (singular, past tense)

  The brothers <u>played</u> soccer on the middle school team. (plural, past tense)

- Compound subjects that are joined by *and* need the plural form of the verb.

  Tara and Cheryl <u>walk</u> to school.

  My brothers and I <u>walk</u> to school.

© Gary Robert Muschla

3.18 What a Hoot!

This large owl has a wingspan of about five feet. It is found in much of North and South America. Sometimes it is called a hoot owl because of its deep call. What is the actual name of this owl?

To answer the question, complete each sentence below with the correct present-tense form of the verb. Choose your answers from the verbs after each sentence. Write the letter of each answer in the space above its sentence number at the bottom of the page. You will need to divide the letters into words.

1. This animal _____ during the night.
   E. hunt   O. hunts

2. Owls _____ their nests at nightfall.
   A. leave   S. leaves

3. An owl's big eyes _____ for prey in the night.
   N. look   S. looks

4. An owl _____ swiftly through the darkness.
   E. fly   D. flies

5. It _____ small birds, animals, and insects.
   T. eat   H. eats

6. Owls _____ in most parts of the world.
   R. live   C. lives

7. On some nights I _____ the hoot of an owl.
   T. hear   C. hears

8. My sister _____ for the owl, too.
   S. listen   G. listens

9. She and I _____ learning about wildlife.
   E. enjoy   R. enjoys

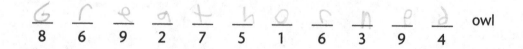

G	r	e	a	t	h	o	r	n	e	d	owl
8	6	9	2	7	5	1	6	3	9	4	

© Gary Robert Muschla

Verbs

72

3.19 Sports Fans

In 1895, W. G. Morgan invented this game. What game did he invent?

To answer the question, complete each sentence below with the correct present-tense form of the verb. Choose your answers from the verbs after each sentence. Write the letter of each answer in the space above its sentence number at the bottom of the page.

1. My family _____ all kinds of sports.
   M. like   E. likes

2. My brothers _____ baseball, basketball, and soccer.
   L. play   C. plays

3. My sister _____ softball and soccer.
   S. love   L. loves

4. My mother and father _____ for exercise each day.
   B. walk   N. walks

5. Sometimes they _____ hiking and bicycling.
   O. go   A. goes

6. I _____ hockey the best of any sport.
   Y. enjoy   S. enjoys

7. We _____ sports events on TV.
   L. watch   R. watches

8. My father and I never _____ a championship game.
   A. miss   H. misses

9. My mom _____ at our love of sports.
   S. smile   L. smiles

10. She _____ a lot about sports.
    B. know   V. knows

 V   O   L   L   e   Y   B   a   L   L
___ ___ ___ ___ ___ ___ ___ ___ ___ ___
10   5   2   7   1   6   4   8   3   9

© Gary Robert Muschla

Verbs

3.20 E. L. Konigsburg

E. L. Konigsburg is the author of *From the Mixed-Up Files of Mrs. Basil E. Frankweiler.* What do the initials *E. L.* stand for?

To answer the question, complete each sentence below with the correct present-tense form of the verb. Choose your answers from the verbs after each sentence. Write the letter of each answer in the space above its sentence number at the bottom of the page. The first letter of the author's name is given.

1. Many authors _____ initials instead of their full names.
   N. use   S. uses

2. Instead of their own name, some writers _____ "pen" names.
   O. choose   I. chooses

3. They _____ stories under a name other than their own.
   A. write   M. writes

4. I _____ at least one novel every two weeks.
   L. read   E. reads

5. My best friend Leandra _____ a novel every week.
   O. finish   I. finishes

6. Leandra _____ to a book club.
   E. belong   B. belongs

7. She and I _____ the best stories.
   L. discuss   W. discusses

8. My mother _____ me about some of her favorite books.
   J. tell   L. tells

9. She _____ books from the library.
   J. borrow   E. borrows

E   L   a   i   n   e   L   a   B   L
7   3   5   1   9   4   2   6   8

© Gary Robert Muschla

Verbs

Regular and Irregular Verbs

Verbs have different forms. Three common verb forms are the present, the past, and the past participle.

Most verbs are known as *regular verbs*. Their past and past participle forms are made by adding *-d* or *-ed* to the present form. The past participle needs the helping verbs *have, has,* or *had*. Here are some examples:

Present	Past	Past Participle
walk	walked	(have, has, had) walked
jump	jumped	(have, has, had) jumped
hike	hiked	(have, has, had) hiked
sip	sipped	(have, has, had) sipped
cry	cried	(have, has, had) cried

Some verbs are known as *irregular verbs*. The past and past participle forms of irregular verbs do not end in *-d* or *-ed*. They may change their spelling, or they may not change at all. Here are some examples:

Present	Past	Past Participle
begin	began	(have, has, had) begun
see	saw	(have, has, had) seen
come	came	(have, has, had) come
give	gave	(have, has, had) given
hit	hit	(have, has, had) hit
know	knew	(have, has, had) known
teach	taught	(have, has, had) taught

Learning the forms of irregular verbs will help you use them correctly.

© Gary Robert Muschla

3.21 Gateway to a New Life

Opened in 1892, this place welcomed millions of immigrants to America. What was the name of this place?

To answer the question, match the present-tense form of the irregular verb on the left with its past-tense form on the right. Write the letter of the past form in the space above the verb's number at the bottom of the page. You will need to divide the letters into words.

Present	Past	
1. run	I. runned	A. ran
2. take	M. taked	S. took
3. fly	I. flew	Y. flyed
4. eat	A. eated	I. ate
5. go	N. went	R. goed
6. choose	W. choosed	L. chose
7. see	G. seed	S. saw
8. give	P. gived	L. gave
9. draw	D. drew	Y. drawed
10. begin	E. began	N. beganned
11. write	L. wrote	E. writ

$\underline{e}$ $\underline{L}$ $\underline{L}$ $\underline{i}$ $\underline{s}$ $\underline{i}$ $\underline{s}$ $\underline{L}$ $\underline{a}$ $\underline{n}$ $\underline{d}$
  10   11   6   3   7   4   2   8   1   5   9

© Gary Robert Muschla

Verbs

3.22 Big Ears

With ears about three feet wide and five feet long, this adult animal has the biggest ears on earth. What animal is this?

To answer the question, match the present-tense form of the irregular verb on the left with its past-tense form on the right. Write the letter of the past form in the space above the verb's number at the bottom of the page. You will need to divide the letters into words.

Present   **Past**

1. bring   C. brought   H. brung

2. grow   I. grew   E. growed

3. do   H. doed   L. did

4. teach   S. teached   F. taught

5. know   W. knewed   H. knew

6. sit   I. set   R. sat

7. swim   T. swam   L. swimmed

8. ride   C. rided   R. rode

9. speak   S. spoked   N. spoke

10. sing   A. sang   W. singed

11. make   O. maked   E. made

A F r i C a n e L e P h a n t
10 4 6 2 1 10 9 11 3 11 8 5 10 9 7

© Gary Robert Muschla

Verbs

3.23 Men on the Moon

On July 20, 1969, Neil A. Armstrong became the first man to walk on the moon. A second astronaut soon joined him. What is the name of the second man to walk on the moon?

To answer the question, complete each sentence below with the correct form of the irregular verb. Choose your answers from the verbs after the sentence. Write the letter of each answer in the space above its sentence number at the bottom of the page.

1. People _____ about going to the moon for a long time.
   E. thinked   L. thought

2. In 1969, American astronauts _____ to the moon.
   N. flown   R. flew

3. They _____ a safe landing on the surface.
   W. made   M. maked

4. The astronauts _____ many pictures of the moon's surface.
   A. took   J. taked

5. They _____ several experiments.
   J. done   E. did

6. They _____ Earth in space more than 240,000 miles away.
   I. saw   A. seen

7. The astronauts _____ back to Earth safely.
   D. came   A. comed

8. They _____ samples of moon rocks and soil back with them.
   D. brung   N. brought

e D w i n   e.   a L D r i n
5 7 3 6 8   5   4 1 7 2 6 8

Verbs

© Gary Robert Muschla

Two Special Verbs: *Be* and *Have*

Be and *have* are special verbs. They may be used alone or as helping verbs. They have special forms in order to agree with their subjects.

Be

Here are some examples of subjects with forms of the verb *be*:

Present Form		Past Form
I	am	was
you	are	were
he, she, it	is	was
we, they	are	were
John	is	was

Have

Here are some examples of subjects with forms of the verb *have*:

Present Form		Past Form
I	have	had
you	have	had
he, she, it	has	had
we, they	have	had
Jennifer	has	had

© Gary Robert Muschla

3.24 Small Dog

This breed of dog is thought to be the smallest of all breeds. What is it?

To answer the question, complete each sentence below with the correct verb. Choose your answers from the verbs after the sentence. Write the letter of each answer in the space above its sentence number at the bottom of the page.

1. Our school _____ an animal show every year.
   K. have   I. has

2. Dogs, cats, birds, and other animals _____ the stars of the show.
   E. is   U. are

3. Aimee and her sister _____ a pet cat.
   N. has   H. have

4. That cat _____ the fluffiest cat at the show.
   A. is   O. are

5. Last year my dog _____ the winner of the Biggest Dog Award.
   U. was   I. were

6. He _____ an Irish setter.
   H. is   E. are

7. Lila's turtles _____ the smallest animals at the show.
   W. was   H. were

8. I _____ always curious to see all the animals.
   T. is   C. am

9. A snake and a white rabbit _____ the winners for the Most Unusual Pets.
   E. was   A. were

C h i w u a h u a
8 6 1 7 2 4 3 5 9

© Gary Robert Muschla

Verbs

3.25 Searching Everywhere

According to researchers, the average American spends a lot of time during his or her life looking for things. How much time is this?

To answer the question, read each sentence below. Decide if the verbs are used correctly. If a sentence is correct, write the letter for *correct* in the space above its number at the bottom of the page. If a sentence is incorrect, write the letter for *incorrect*. You will need to divide the letters into words.

1. Paulo is always misplacing things.
   N. Correct   W. Incorrect

2. Last month he has lost the keys to his house.
   E. Correct   U. Incorrect

3. He were searching everywhere for them.
   M. Correct   T. Incorrect

4. He have never lost his keys before.
   O. Correct   E. Incorrect

5. Unlike Paulo, his sister and brother be very responsible.
   N. Correct   B. Incorrect

6. They have never lost anything important.
   O. Correct   I. Incorrect

7. Yesterday Paulo has misplaced his math homework.
   H. Correct   R. Incorrect

8. His brother and sister were helping him look for it.
   Y. Correct   O. Incorrect

9. Paulo's homework was in his science book.
   A. Correct   T. Incorrect

$\overline{}$ $\overline{}$ $\overline{}$ $\overline{}$ $\overline{}$ $\overline{}$ $\overline{}$ $\overline{}$ $\overline{}$ $\overline{}$ $\overline{}$ $\overline{}$

9   5   6   2   3   6   1   4   8   4   9   7

© Gary Robert Muschla

Verbs

3.26 Warriors and Explorers

From about A.D. 800 to 1100, fierce warriors attacked parts of Europe. What were these warriors called?

To answer the question, read the paragraph below. Decide if the underlined words are verbs or verb phrases. Some of the underlined words are *not* verbs or verb phrases. Start with the first sentence. Then write the letter beneath each correct verb or verb phrase in order in the spaces at the bottom of the page.

About 1,200 years ago, warriors from northern Europe <u>sailed southward</u>. They
                                                                       P

<u>came from</u> the countries of Denmark, Norway, and Sweden. Today these countries
   I

<u>are called</u> Scandinavia. The warriors <u>were</u> <u>fearless</u> sailors. At first they <u>raided</u> the
    V   I   S   K

coasts of Europe. Then some of them <u>sailed westward</u>. They <u>discovered</u> Iceland and
                                        U   I

Greenland. They even <u>reached</u> North America. This <u>was about</u> 500 years before
                   N   E

Columbus. Their adventures <u>were told</u> in stories. These stories <u>are known</u> as sagas.
                            G   S

__ __ __ __ __ __ __ __ __ __

© Gary Robert Muschla

3.27 Three Special Sets of Letters

Only three sets of letters on a standard computer keyboard are in order. What are these three sets of letters?

To answer the question, complete each sentence below with the correct form of the verb. Choose your answers from the verbs after each sentence. Write the letter of each answer in the space above its sentence number at the bottom of the page.

1. Mrs. Harris _____ computers in our school.

    R. teach   K. teaches

2. She _____ her students how to type on a computer keyboard.

    G. taught   M. teached

3. My friend Debbie _____ one of her students.

    P. is   L. am

4. Debbie _____ type much faster now.

    L. can   N. could

5. She _____ words very quickly.

    Q. type   H. types

6. All of the students _____ improved their typing skills.

    E. has   O. have

7. I _____ able to type much faster now, too.

    J. am   H. is

8. I _____ my book report on my computer.

    P. writ   F. wrote

$\overline{\quad}$ $\overline{\quad}$ $\overline{\quad}$ $\overline{\quad}$ $\overline{\quad}$ $\overline{\quad}$ $\overline{\quad}$ $\overline{\quad}$

  8   2   5   7   1   4   6   3

© Gary Robert Muschla

Verbs

3.28 Great Explorer

Samuel de Champlain was one of Canada's most famous explorers. Historians have given him a special title. What is this title?

To answer the question, read each sentence below. Find the verb or verb phrase. If the verb or verb phrase is used correctly, write the letter for *correct* in the space above its sentence number at the bottom of the page. If the verb or verb phrase is used incorrectly, write the letter for *incorrect*. You will need to divide the letters into words.

1. Samuel de Champlain is born in France about 1567.
   E. Correct   W. Incorrect

2. He sailed to the New World in 1599.
   T. Correct   A. Incorrect

3. In 1603, he make his first trip to North America.
   L. Correct   C. Incorrect

4. He explore the St. Lawrence River.
   X. Correct   O. Incorrect

5. He helped start a new settlement.
   H. Correct   T. Incorrect

6. This settlement became the city of Quebec.
   N. Correct   U. Incorrect

7. Samuel de Champlain build a trading post at Montreal.
   R. Correct   E. Incorrect

8. He spent many more years exploring Canada.
   A. Correct   R. Incorrect

9. In 1633, he was made governor of French lands in Canada.
   F. Correct   N. Incorrect

10. Samuel de Champlain dies in 1635.
    E. Correct   R. Incorrect

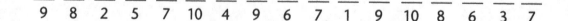

__ __ __ __ __ __ __ __ __ __ __ __ __ __ __ __ __
9   8   2   5   7 10   4   9   6   7   1   9 10   8   6   3   7

Verbs

© Gary Robert Muschla

3.29 Step up to the Plate

The first professional baseball team was organized in 1869. In what city and state did the team play?

To answer the question, read each sentence below. Match the underlined word or phrase with the term that best describes it. Choose your answers from the terms that follow the sentences. Write the letter of each answer in the space above its sentence number at the bottom of the page. You will need to divide the letters into words.

1. One of our country's favorite sports is <u>baseball</u>.

2. Baseball <u>is played</u> in many parts of the world.

3. The first professional baseball team <u>was</u> the Red Stockings.

4. I <u>play</u> second base for my team.

5. Our coach <u>taught</u> us the rules of the game.

6. In our last game I hit the <u>ball</u> hard.

7. In my opinion, baseball is <u>great</u>.

Answers

O. Action Verb

A. Linking Verb

I. Irregular Verb

T. Verb Phrase

H. Noun After Linking Verb

N. Adjective After Linking Verb

C. Direct Object

___ ___ ___ ___ ___ ___ ___ ___ ___ ___ ___ ___ ___ ___
6   5   7   6   5   7   7   3   2   5   4   1   5   4

© Gary Robert Muschla

Verbs

Pronouns

Pronouns are words that replace nouns. There are many different kinds of pronouns.

The tip sheets and worksheets that follow address the different pronouns and their usage. The first tip sheet of this part introduces pronouns. Worksheets 4.1 through 4.4 concentrate on identifying pronouns. Three tip sheets and Worksheets 4.5 through 4.9 cover subject and object pronouns. One tip sheet and Worksheets 4.10 through 4.12 focus on possessive pronouns, while a tip sheet and Worksheets 4.13 and 4.14 address pronoun contractions. Worksheet 4.15 addresses antecedents, and Worksheets 4.16 through 4.18 conclude Part 4 with reviews.

Pronouns

. . . .

Pronouns are words that take the place of nouns. Two of the most important kinds of pronouns follow.

- *Personal pronouns* take the place of persons, places, things, or ideas. They may be singular or plural.

Singular	Plural
I, me	we, us
you	you
he, she, him, her, it	they, them

- *Possessive pronouns* are personal pronouns that show *who* or *what* owns something. They may be singular or plural.

Singular	Plural
my, mine	our, ours
your, yours	your, yours
his, her, hers, its	their, theirs

© Gary Robert Muschla

4.1 Fairy Tale Author

This author wrote "The Ugly Duckling," "The Snow Queen," and "The Little Mermaid." Who was he?

To answer the question, find the pronoun in each set of words below. Write the letter of the pronoun in the space above its line number at the bottom of the page.

1. U. city	H. and	T. we	R. take
2. M. plane	D. her	V. are	T. know
3. D. pretty	E. friend	C. our	O. trip
4. I. they	W. learn	N. after	G. word
5. A. place	I. been	S. you	C. an
6. P. along	R. happy	H. me	N. coast
7. R. his	E. for	W. exciting	P. small
8. L. sunny	E. I	Y. or	S. tells
9. I. finish	M. work	A. it	O. with
10. H. storm	N. their	E. about	B. done

__ __ __ __   __ __ __ __ __ __ __ __ __
6 9 10 5   3 6 7 4 5 1 4 9 10

__ __ __ __ __ __ __ __
9 10 2 8 7 5 8 10

© Gary Robert Muschla

4.2 Tinkering Around

This man invented Tinkertoys. Who was he?

To answer the question, find the pronoun in each set of words below. Write the letter of the pronoun in the space above its line number at the bottom of the page.

1. U. food	R. my	I. always	E. dessert
2. I. chilly	C. the	H. delightful	J. us
3. N. plan	F. was	U. he	M. is
4. A. beautiful	E. to	I. town	S. them
5. P. him	W. day	V. brings	R. in
6. D. make	C. mine	L. cook	A. cold
7. L. its	A. state	O. no	S. suppose
8. S. but	H. your	E. very	M. enter
9. H. tired	O. country	A. she	C. hand
10. R. interesting	F. night	E. hers	T. sun

___ ___ ___ ___ ___ ___ ___   ___ ___ ___ ___ ___ ___
6   8   9   1   7   10 4   5   9   2   10 9   3

© Gary Robert Muschla

4.3 Hot Dogs

Most Americans like hot dogs. In the past, hot dogs had many different names. One of these names was based on a real breed of dog. What was this name for hot dogs?

To answer the question, read each sentence below. Find the pronoun. Choose your answers from the underlined words. Write the letter of the pronoun in the space above its sentence number at the bottom of the page.

1. Sheila and her family had a picnic last Sunday.
       N G   R

2. They went to a nearby park.
     C   S   D

3. Sheila's brother helped their father carry the cooler from the car.
                     E   S   B

4. Uncle Bill and Aunt Janet joined them at the park.
                   L   N   C

5. "I brought the salad and dessert," said Aunt Janet.
    U H   N

6. "Did you also bring paper plates?" asked Sheila's mother.
       A O   E

7. "Yes," said Aunt Janet. "We have napkins, too."
          H M   I

8. "She never forgets anything," said Uncle Bill.
     S   N   D

9. "Please hand me the plates," said Sheila's mother.
     O   D S

___ ___ ___ ___ ___ ___ ___ ___ ___   ___ ___ ___ ___ ___ ___ ___ ___
9   6   2   7   8   7   5   4   9   8   6   5   8   6   1   3   8

© Gary Robert Muschla

4.4 Flat State

This is the flattest state in the United States. Its highest point is only 345 feet above sea level. What state is it?

To answer the question, read each sentence below. Replace each underlined word or group of words with a pronoun that makes a correct sentence. Choose your answers from the pronouns listed after the sentences. Write the letter of each pronoun in the space above its sentence number at the bottom of the page. Some pronouns will not be used.

1. <u>Jenna and Eduardo</u> were learning about the states.

2. <u>Jenna</u> was born in Ohio.

3. <u>Eduardo</u> was born in New York.

4. <u>Eduardo's</u> mother and father once lived in New Jersey.

5. <u>Jenna's</u> family originally came from Pennsylvania.

6. Mrs. Riley, the librarian, helped <u>Jenna and Eduardo</u> find information.

7. <u>The information</u> was very interesting and helpful.

Answers

I. he	O. she	D. her	A. they	T. us
L. them	R. his	N. we	F. it	J. their

‾‾ ‾‾ ‾‾ ‾‾ ‾‾ ‾‾ ‾‾
7   6   2   4   3   5   1

© Gary Robert Muschla

Subject Pronouns

The subject of a sentence tells whom or what the sentence is about. Pronouns can be used as subjects of sentences.

- The *subject pronouns* are *I, you, he, she, it, we,* and *they.*

  I watched a movie last night.

  You won the contest.

  He is a great soccer player.

  She plays the violin.

  It (the book) is on the desk.

  We will go to the library.

  They went to a basketball game.

- Subject pronouns are also used after linking verbs.

  The student of the month was she.

  The two new members of the band were Martin and he.

© Gary Robert Muschla

4.5 Word Game

One of the early names of this popular game was Criss-Cross Words. Its name was changed long ago. What is the name of this game today?

To answer the question, read the story below. Decide if the underlined pronouns are subject pronouns. Start with the first sentence. Then write the letters beneath the subject pronouns in order in the spaces at the bottom of the page.

Saturday afternoon was rainy. Serena and her friends were disappointed. They
                                                   C   S

had planned to play soccer.

Jason looked out the window at the rain. He frowned. There seemed to be little
                                          C

for them to do.
    H

"What can we do?" asked Serena.
            R

"I don't know," said Jason, shaking his head.
 A   E

"Do you have a new CD?" he asked her.
    B   T

"Yes," she told them. "We can listen to music."
       B   R   L

"That sounds like a good idea to me," Meg said.
                                    U

They listened to music for the rest of the day.
 E

___ ___ ___ ___ ___ ___ ___ ___

© Gary Robert Muschla

Object Pronouns

. . . .

Pronouns can be used as objects in a sentence.

- The *object pronouns* are *me, you, him, her, it, us,* and *them.*

- Object pronouns follow action verbs. They receive the action of the verb.

  Tess called <u>him</u> yesterday.

  Sammi asked <u>her</u> about the tickets.

  John left <u>it</u> (the umbrella) home.

  Mia sent <u>them</u> a package.

- Object pronouns may also follow prepositions. Prepositions are words such as *at, before, for, into, to,* and *with.*

  I sent the package to <u>you</u>.

  Do these keys belong to <u>him</u>?

  Is that book for <u>me</u>?

  Tom is driving with <u>us</u>.

© Gary Robert Muschla

. . . .

4.6 Moving Along . . . Slowly

Many animal experts believe that the three-toed sloth is the slowest moving mammal on land. About how far does the sloth go in a minute?

To answer the question, read the story below. Decide if the underlined pronouns are object pronouns. Start with the first sentence. Then write the letters beneath the object pronouns in order in the spaces at the bottom of the page. You will need to divide the letters into words.

Jordan and <u>his</u> father like hiking. Last week, for the first time, <u>they</u> took Jordan's
         O   N

younger sister Shiloh with <u>them</u>. <u>They</u> packed <u>their</u> lunches and plenty of water.
                            S   U   N

Shiloh helped Jordan load the car. She handed a knapsack to <u>him</u>. Jordan
                                                                   I

placed <u>it</u> in the trunk.
     X

"Here," <u>his</u> father said to Jordan. "This is for <u>you</u>."
        E   F

<u>He</u> handed Jordan a compass.
O

"<u>You</u> will have to keep <u>us</u> heading in the right direction," <u>he</u> said.
 R   E   M

"What about <u>me</u>?" asked Shiloh. "What can <u>I</u> do?"
          E   S

"<u>You</u> can help, too," <u>their</u> father said. He gave a compass to <u>her</u>.
 J   P   T

___   ___   ___   ___   ___   ___   ___

© Gary Robert Muschla

Two Special Pronouns: *I* and *Me*

I is a subject pronoun. *Me* is an object pronoun. To use these pronouns correctly, remember these tips:

- *I* can replace a noun that is a subject of a sentence. *I* can also follow a linking verb.

  I went to the library. (subject of sentence)

  Shane and I went to the library. (subject of sentence)

  The spelling bee champion was I. (follows linking verb *was*)

- *Me* can replace a noun that follows an action verb or a preposition. A preposition is a word such as *at, before, for, from,* or *into.*

  Susan called me last night. (follows action verb *called*)

  Tom gave me the report. (follows action verb *gave*)

  The package was for me. (follows preposition *for*)

- Never use *me* as a subject.

  Laurie and me are best friends. (incorrect)

  Laurie and I are best friends. (correct)

© Gary Robert Muschla

4.7 Big Eyes

This mammal has the biggest eyes of all mammals. They are about five inches in diameter. What is the name of this mammal?

To answer the question, complete each sentence below with the correct subject or object pronoun. Choose your answers from the pronouns after each sentence. Write the letter of each answer in the space above its sentence number at the bottom of the page. You will need to divide the letters into words.

1. My big sister Amy took _____ to a museum last week.
   T. I   A. me

2. She and _____ learned much about nature.
   E. I   P. me

3. Amy and _____ visited all of the exhibits.
   W. I   R. me

4. The exhibits on mammals were most interesting to _____.
   C. I   E. me

5. A guide showed Amy and _____ around.
   F. I   L. me

6. _____ asked our guide many questions.
   L. I   N. Me

7. The guide told Amy and _____ many fascinating facts.
   E. I   U. me

8. The most interested visitors were Amy and _____.
   B. I   E. me

9. _____ enjoyed visiting the museum.
   H. I   E. Me

__	__	__	__	__	__	__	__	__
8	5	7	2	3	9	1	6	4

© Gary Robert Muschla

4.8 Brothers and Sisters

What is a name (other than brothers and sisters) for people who have the same parents?

To answer the question, complete each sentence below with the correct subject or object pronoun. Choose your answers from the pronouns after each sentence. Write the letter of each answer in the space above its sentence number at the bottom of the page.

1. Mark and _____ are twins.
   S. I   D. me

2. Some people have trouble telling _____ apart.
   R. we   I. us

3. But _____ can't fool our parents.
   I. we   E. us

4. _____ always recognize the two of us.
   G. They   T. Them

5. There are a lot of differences between Mark and _____.
   L. I   B. me

6. For _____, baseball is the most exciting game.
   U. he   N. him

7. But _____ like soccer best.
   S. I   R. me

8. To most people, _____ seem more alike than different.
   L. we   T. us

___ ___ ___ ___ ___ ___ ___ ___
 7   3   5   8   2   6   4   1

© Gary Robert Muschla

4.9 Dr. Seuss

Just about everybody knows of the stories of Dr. Seuss. What was Dr. Seuss's full name?

To answer the question, read each sentence below. If the pronouns in the sentence are used correctly, write the letter for *correct* in the space above the sentence number at the bottom of the page. If a pronoun is used incorrectly, write the letter for *incorrect*. Part of his full name is provided.

1. My sister Samantha and me love to read.
   R. Correct   D. Incorrect

2. Her and I especially like the stories of Dr. Seuss.
   Y. Correct   I. Incorrect

3. I think *The Cat in the Hat* is his best book.
   L. Correct   A. Incorrect

4. She agrees with me.
   H. Correct   M. Incorrect

5. Our friend Marci gave us some books about Dr. Seuss.
   S. Correct   N. Incorrect

6. Samantha and I read the books.
   R. Correct   K. Incorrect

7. Afterward I returned them to she.
   E. Correct   T. Incorrect

8. My mother gave Samantha and I books for our birthdays.
   V. Correct   E. Incorrect

9. We have many of his books.
   G. Correct   M. Incorrect

10. Me and Samantha think Dr. Seuss is a great author.
    J. Correct   O. Incorrect

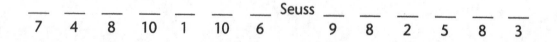

___ ___ ___ ___ ___ ___ ___ Seuss ___ ___ ___ ___ ___ ___
 7   4   8   10   1   10   6   9   8   2   5   8   3

© Gary Robert Muschla

Possessive Pronouns

Possessive pronouns show who or what owns something. They take the place of possessive nouns. Unlike possessive nouns, possessive pronouns do not have apostrophes.

- The following are possessive pronouns: *my, mine, your, yours, his, her, hers, its, our, ours, their,* and *theirs.*

- Some possessive pronouns are used with nouns in sentences: *my, your, his, her, its, our,* and *their.*

    Your pen is on the table.

    Where are my books?

    He found his book.

    Her car is in the driveway.

    Their house is on Main Street.

- Some possessive pronouns are used alone: *mine, yours, his, hers, its, ours,* and *theirs.*

    That math book is his.

    That coat is hers.

    That folder is yours.

    Hers is on the desk.

    That house is theirs.

- Do not confuse possessive pronouns with pronoun contractions.

Possessive Pronoun	Contraction
your	you're (you are)
its	it's (it is)
their	they're (they are)
whose	who's (who is)

© Gary Robert Muschla

4.10 Astronauts

The word *astronauts* comes from ancient Greek. What is the original meaning of *astronauts*?

To answer the question, find the possessive pronoun in each set of words below. Write the letter of the possessive pronoun in the space above its line number at the bottom of the page. You will need to divide the letters into words.

1. S. me	E. his	L. anyone	R. each
2. N. both	H. she	T. I	I. their
3. R. its	D. we	P. what	S. none
4. E. they're	N. some	A. yours	R. him
5. F. ours	S. it's	E. them	H. every
6. N. you	H. her	L. anything	E. where
7. O. they	H. all	D. few	O. mine
8. C. many	T. your	H. it	Q. someone
9. D. these	K. nothing	S. that	L. hers
10. W. you're	S. my	C. nobody	R. who

__ __ __ __ __ __ __ __ __ __ __ __ __ __ __ __ __

10 4 2 9 7 3 10 7 5 8 6 1 10 8 4 3 10

© Gary Robert Muschla

4.11 American Composer

A composer is a songwriter. This American composer wrote some of America's most popular songs, including "God Bless America." Who was he?

To answer the question, complete each sentence below with the correct possessive pronoun. Choose your answers from the pronouns after each sentence. Write the letter of each answer in the space above its sentence number at the bottom of the page.

1. The school band was practicing for _____ winter concert.
   E. they're   L. their

2. I am a member of _____ school's band.
   V. my   H. mine

3. Of all the school bands in the county, _____ is the best.
   K. our   G. ours

4. My friend Natalie could not find _____ flute.
   B. her   L. hers

5. "Is that _____ on that table?" I asked.
   R. your   N. yours

6. "No," she said. "My flute is in _____ case."
   E. its   X. it's

7. "That one is _____," said Rachel.
   D. my   R. mine

8. _____ teacher, Mrs. Kelly, called for quiet.
   I. Our   T. Ours

9. "Everyone, please give me _____ attention," she said.
   I. your   B. you're

___ ___ ___ ___ ___ ___   ___ ___ ___ ___ ___ ___
 9   7   2   8   5   3   4   6   7   1   8   5

4.12 Plenty of Prairie

A prairie is mostly flat land covered with tall grass. This state has so much prairie that only about 1 percent of it has forest. This is less than any other state. What state is this?

To answer the question, read each sentence below. Find the possessive pronouns and decide if they are used correctly. If the possessive pronouns are used correctly, write the letter for *correct* in the space above the sentence number at the bottom of the page. If a possessive pronoun in a sentence is used incorrectly, write the letter for *incorrect*. You will need to divide the letters into words.

1. Carlos and his family are moving.
   H. Correct   N. Incorrect

2. They're new home is in Oregon.
   W. Correct   K. Incorrect

3. Carlos and his sister helped pack their family's car.
   O. Correct   K. Incorrect

4. His suitcase was bigger than his sister's.
   A. Correct   S. Incorrect

5. But hers had more room inside.
   R. Correct   U. Incorrect

6. "Where is the box with you're CDs and videos?" Carlos's father asked him.
   R. Correct   D. Incorrect

7. "Its already in the car next to my suitcase," said Carlos.
   M. Correct   T. Incorrect

8. "Mine things are already packed, too," said his sister.
   S. Correct   N. Incorrect

___ ___ ___ ___ ___ ___ ___ ___ ___ ___ ___
 8   3   5   7   1   6   4   2   3   7   4

© Gary Robert Muschla

Pronoun Contractions

A pronoun contraction is the short form of two words. It is made up of a pronoun and a verb. An apostrophe is used to show where a letter or letters have been left out.

- Many subject pronouns form contractions with verbs. Here are common examples:

I am—I'm	you have—you've	we will—we'll
you are—you're	we have—we've	they will—they'll
she is—she's	they have—they've	I had—I'd
he is—he's	I will—I'll	you had—you'd
it is—it's	you will—you'll	he had—he'd
we are—we're	he will—he'll	she had—she'd
they are—they're	she will—she'll	we had—we'd
I have—I've	it will—it'll	they had—they'd

© Gary Robert Muschla

4.13 Born on the Fourth of July

This president was born on July 4, 1872. Who was he?
To answer the question, match the words on the left with the contraction they make on the right. Write the letter of each answer in the space above the word's number at the bottom of the page. You will need to divide the letters into words.

Words	Contractions
1. I am	D. she'll
2. you are	I. he'd
3. she will	L. I've
4. we have	O. you've
5. they are	G. we'll
6. he would	E. we've
7. you have	C. he's
8. we will	N. I'm
9. he is	V. they're
10. I have	A. you're

— — — — — — — — — — — — — —
9   2   10   5   6   1   9   7   7   10   6   3   8   4

© Gary Robert Muschla

4.14 Discoverer of Antibiotics

Antibiotics are medicines that fight germs that cause infections. Dr. Alexander Fleming discovered the first antibiotic in 1928. Which antibiotic did he discover?

To answer the question, match the words on the left with the contraction they make on the right. Write the letter of each answer in the space above the word's number at the bottom of the page.

Words	**Contractions**
1. you would	P. it's
2. she is	I. I'd
3. they have	L. I'll
4. you are	N. you'll
5. they had	L. they've
6. I will	I. he'd
7. he had	E. you're
8. it is	I. they'd
9. you will	C. you'd
10. I had	N. she's

___ ___ ___ ___ ___ ___ ___ ___ ___ ___
 8   4   9   5   1   7   6   3   10   2

© Gary Robert Muschla

4.15 Animals with Great Memories

These animals have excellent memories. It is said that they never forget. What animals are these?

To answer the question, read each sentence below. Find the word that each underlined pronoun replaces. In the parentheses after the sentence, a letter is called for. Find this letter in the word the pronoun replaces. Write this letter in the space above the sentence number at the bottom of the page. The first one is done for you.

1. The <u>members</u> of the Smith family say <u>they</u> are forgetful. (seventh letter)

2. Eddie is always misplacing <u>his</u> things. (first letter)

3. Eddie's mother misplaced <u>her</u> car keys yesterday. (third letter)

4. Yesterday morning, Eddie's father couldn't find <u>his</u> wallet. (second letter)

5. Liz explains that <u>she</u> always seems to lose things. (first letter)

6. Eddie's aunt forgets where <u>she</u> puts things, too. (third letter)

7. Even Happy, the family's puppy, loses <u>his</u> toys. (first letter)

8. Only Grandpa never loses any of <u>his</u> things. (sixth letter)

9. Fortunately, the people in this family always find what <u>they</u> are looking for. (second letter)

$$\frac{\quad}{2} \quad \frac{\quad}{5} \quad \frac{\quad}{9} \quad \frac{\quad}{8} \quad \frac{\quad}{7} \quad \frac{\quad}{4} \quad \frac{\quad}{6} \quad \frac{\quad}{3} \quad \frac{S}{1}$$

© Gary Robert Muschla

4.16 Dangerous Fish

To many skin divers, this fish is more dangerous than a shark. What fish is this?

To answer the question, read each sentence below. Find the pronoun. Choose your answers from the underlined words. Write the letter of each answer in the space above its sentence number at the bottom of the page.

1. Lenny is learning <u>about</u> the oceans in <u>his</u> <u>science</u> class.
                 E   A   U

2. <u>He</u> is <u>very</u> interested <u>in</u> sharks.
  A   O   T

3. "A <u>lot</u> of people <u>are</u> afraid of <u>them</u>," said Lenny.
    H   N   C

4. Sara and <u>her</u> friend <u>did</u> a <u>report</u> on sharks.
         R   M   W

5. "<u>We</u> learned that <u>most</u> sharks <u>can</u> be dangerous," Sara said.
   D   K   T

6. "But <u>not</u> all sharks <u>are</u> dangerous," <u>she</u> said.
       H   C   A

7. Mrs. Wallace, <u>their</u> teacher, <u>told</u> the class <u>about</u> whale sharks.
            U   E   P

8. "<u>They</u> <u>are</u> harmless to <u>people</u>," Mrs. Wallace said.
  B G   O

9. The teacher held <u>up</u> a picture <u>and</u> showed <u>it</u> to the class.
          T   M   R

___ ___ ___ ___ ___ ___ ___ ___ ___
 8   2   9   4   1   3   7   5   6

© Gary Robert Muschla

4.17 Tiny Mammal

This mammal lives in Thailand, a country in southeast Asia. It is thought to be the world's smallest mammal. It weighs less than a penny. What is it?

To answer the question, match each pronoun on the left with its most accurate label on the right. Write the letter of each answer in the space above the pronoun's number at the bottom of the page.

1. their   E. Personal Pronoun, Singular, Subject

2. we   T. Personal Pronoun, Singular, Object

3. mine   M. Personal Pronoun, Plural, Subject

4. we've   U. Personal Pronoun, Plural, Object

5. she   A. Possessive Pronoun, Singular

6. them   L. Possessive Pronoun, Plural

7. him   B. Pronoun Contraction

8. I

9. it's

10. you'd

11. he

12. I'm

$$\overline{}\ \overline{}\ \overline{}\ \overline{}\ \overline{}\ \overline{}\ \overline{}\ \overline{}\ \overline{}\quad\overline{}\ \overline{}\ \overline{}$$
10   6   2   12   1   8   4   11   5   9   3   7

© Gary Robert Muschla

4.18 Pets

Pronouns

Millions of people around the world have pets. In the United States, dogs, cats, birds, hamsters, and fish are popular pets. In Japan, a particular insect is often kept as a pet. What insect is a popular pet in Japan?

To answer the question, read each sentence below. Decide if the pronouns are used correctly. If the pronouns are used correctly, write the letter for *correct* in the space above the sentence number at the bottom of the page. If a pronoun in a sentence is used incorrectly, write the letter for *incorrect*.

1. Ashley and her sister Megan take care of Duke, they're dog.
   E. Correct   I. Incorrect

2. They feed him and play with him.
   E. Correct   A. Incorrect

3. "You and me should give Duke a bath," said Ashley to Megan.
   N. Correct   S. Incorrect

4. "I don't think he will like that," said Megan.
   R. Correct   P. Incorrect

5. "We can try," said Ashley. "You're job will be to hold him."
   R. Correct   T. Incorrect

6. Her and Megan got a big tub and filled it with water.
   D. Correct   C. Incorrect

7. They quickly found that Duke didn't like getting his feet wet.
   C. Correct   S. Incorrect

8. Their mother came to help them.
   K. Correct   N. Incorrect

   ___   ___   ___   ___   ___   ___   ___   ___
    7   4   1   6   8   2   5   3

© Gary Robert Muschla

Adjectives

Adjectives are words that modify nouns or pronouns. Adjectives provide details and tell *what kind*, *which one*, *how many*, or *how much*.

The tip sheets and worksheets of this part address various topics and skills related to adjectives. The first tip sheet and Worksheets 5.1 through 5.3 concentrate on identifying adjectives, while Worksheet 5.4 focuses on proper adjectives. The next two tip sheets and Worksheets 5.5 through 5.7 focus on the comparison of adjectives, and Worksheets 5.8 and 5.9 provide reviews.

Adjectives

Adjectives are words that describe a noun or pronoun. There are different kinds of adjectives.

- Most adjectives tell *what kind* or *how many*.

  The <u>chilly</u> rain made me shiver. (what kind)

  <u>Ten</u> inches of snow fell. (how many)

- Adjectives usually come before the nouns they describe. But they can also follow linking verbs.

  The stars were <u>bright</u>.

  The movie was <u>great</u>.

- The words *a, an,* and *the* are special adjectives. They are called *articles*. Use *a* before a noun that starts with a consonant. Use *an* before a noun that starts with a vowel sound. Use *the* before specific persons, places, or things.

  Have <u>a</u> sandwich for lunch.

  Here is <u>an</u> apple for a snack.

  I had <u>the</u> tomato soup for lunch.

- When used before nouns, the words *this, that, these,* and *those* are *demonstrative adjectives. This* and *that* come before singular nouns. *These* and *those* come before plural nouns.

  <u>This</u> book is interesting.

  <u>These</u> books are interesting.

  <u>That</u> tree is tall.

  <u>Those</u> trees are tall.

- *Proper adjectives* are adjectives formed from proper nouns.

Proper Noun	Proper Adjective
America	American students
Mexico	Mexican food
Japan	Japanese cars

© Gary Robert Muschla

5.1 Great Athlete

This woman was an Olympic gold medal winner. She also became a champion golfer. Although she died in 1956, she is still thought to be one of the greatest woman athletes of all time. Who was she?

To answer the question, find the adjective in each set of words below. Write the letter of the adjective in the space above its line number at the bottom of the page.

1. K. field	E. draw	O. chilly	W. from
2. H. thin	A. try	S. line	V. need
3. Y. when	L. moon	C. about	E. clear
4. K. icy	T. and	M. walk	J. night
5. N. windy	M. bring	R. with	E. hill
6. N. star	T. river	S. tall	P. yard
7. V. bird	H. swim	R. branch	I. wonderful
8. J. into	I. forest	Z. snowy	O. animal
9. U. day	A. tiny	O. evening	L. sun
10. B. strong	N. end	C. fish	R. below
11. J. now	D. children	N. there	R. big
12. C. weather	K. begin	D. bright	F. mouth

___ ___ ___ ___   ___ ___ ___ ___ ___ ___ ___ ___
10 9 10 3   12 7 12 11 7 4 6 1 5

___ ___ ___ ___ ___ ___ ___ ___
 8 9 2 9 11 7 9 6

© Gary Robert Muschla

Adjectives

5.2 A Fact About the Cells of Your Body

Individual cells make up your body. A newborn human baby has about twenty-six billion cells. An adult has far more. About how many cells make up an adult human body?

To answer the question, read each sentence below. Find the adjective. Choose your answers from the underlined words. Write the letter beneath the adjective in the space above its sentence number at the bottom of the page. You will need to divide the letters into words.

1. While playing <u>soccer</u>, Jared <u>sprained</u> his <u>left</u> ankle.
                N   S   O

2. His <u>mother</u> drove <u>him</u> to <u>the</u> doctor.
        I   N   Y

3. Dr. Wilson <u>took</u> x-rays of Jared's <u>swollen</u> ankle.
        O   S   L

4. The <u>injury</u> was <u>very</u> <u>painful</u>.
    W   S   N

5. <u>Fortunately</u>, <u>it</u> was only <u>a</u> sprain.
    H   E   R

6. Jared would <u>need</u> to use crutches <u>for</u> a <u>few</u> days.
       N   S   T

7. Dr. Wilson <u>wrapped</u> Jared's ankle <u>in</u> a <u>thick</u> bandage.
       E   A   F

8. Jared would be playing soccer <u>again</u> in <u>about</u> <u>two</u> weeks.
        G   O I

___ ___ ___ ___ ___ ___ ___ ___ ___ ___ ___ ___ ___
7   8   7   6   2   6   5   8   3   3   8   1   4

© Gary Robert Muschla

5.3 Unusual Colony

The capital city of this country was once a place for British prisoners. What country is this?

To answer the question, read the article below. Decide if the underlined words are adjectives. Not all adjectives in the article are underlined. Start with the first sentence. Then write the letters beneath the underlined adjectives in order in the spaces at the bottom of the page.

Deena and her <u>family</u> are going on a <u>great</u> vacation. She and her <u>younger</u> brother
              C   A   U

can't <u>wait</u> to leave. The <u>happy</u> children <u>helped</u> their parents pack <u>big</u> suitcases. They
    L   S   M   T

planned to <u>leave</u> in <u>the</u> morning. They will drive <u>from</u> New York to Florida. It will be <u>a</u>
     I   R   H   A

<u>long</u> trip. Deena hopes that they <u>will</u> have <u>nice</u> weather for their vacation. Everyone is
 L   N   I

looking <u>forward</u> to having a <u>wonderful</u> time.
   S   A

___ ___ ___ ___ ___ ___ ___ ___ ___

Adjectives

© Gary Robert Muschla

5.4 The Civil War

The first shots of the American Civil War were fired in South Carolina on April 12, 1861. Confederate troops attacked Union soldiers. Where did this happen?

To answer the question, match each proper noun with its correct proper adjective. Write the letter of each answer in the space above its number at the bottom of the page.

1. America	R. Amerikan	M. American
2. China	U. Chinas	O. Chinese
3. Mexico	E. Mexican	L. Mexicona
4. Canada	R. Canadien	U. Canadian
5. Japan	R. Japanese	I. Japaneese
6. France	N. Francean	T. French
7. England	T. English	J. Englandern
8. Germany	R. German	K. Germanys
9. Italy	M. Italyan	F. Italian
10. Ireland	G. Irelandin	S. Irish

$\overline{}$ $\overline{}$ $\overline{}$ $\overline{}$ $\overline{}$ $\overline{}$ $\overline{}$ $\overline{}$ $\overline{}$ $\overline{}$
 9   2   8   6   10   4   1   7   3   5

© Gary Robert Muschla

Comparing with Adjectives

Many adjectives have three forms. These forms are used when nouns or pronouns are compared.

- To compare two things, add -er to most adjectives. To compare three or more things, add -est.

  young younger youngest
  tall taller tallest

- For adjectives that end in -e, drop the final -e and add -er or -est.

  large larger largest
  wide wider widest

- For adjectives that end with a consonant and -y, change the -y to -i and add -er or -est.

  happy happier happiest
  early earlier earliest

- For adjectives of one syllable that end with a single vowel and a consonant, double the consonant and add -er or -est.

  wet wetter wettest
  thin thinner thinnest

Here is an example of comparing with adjectives.

The brown puppy is <u>big</u>.

The white puppy is <u>bigger</u> than the brown puppy.

The black puppy is the <u>biggest</u> puppy of the litter.

© Gary Robert Muschla

Special Adjectives and Comparing

With some adjectives of two or more syllables, use *more* or *most* when comparing nouns or pronouns.

- Use *more* to compare two things and *most* to compare three.

serious	more serious	most serious
helpful	more helpful	most helpful
enjoyable	more enjoyable	most enjoyable

  Sara is a <u>helpful</u> person.

  Nan is <u>more helpful</u> than Sara.

  Justine is the <u>most helpful</u> person I know.

- Do not use *more* or *most* with the *-er* or *-est* form of an adjective.

  This tree is <u>more taller</u> than that tree. (incorrect)

  This tree is <u>taller</u> than that tree. (correct)

- The words *good* and *bad* are adjectives. They have special forms.

good	better	best
bad	worse	worst

  John is a <u>good</u> soccer player.

  Martin is a <u>better</u> soccer player than John.

  Tom is the <u>best</u> player on the soccer team.

© Gary Robert Muschla

5.5 Radio Signals

In 1899, Guglielmo Marconi sent the first international radio signals. What country did he send the signals from? And what country did he send the signals to?

To answer the question, find the correct adjective form. Choose the correct form from the words following the numbered adjective. Only one of the choices for each adjective will be correct. Write the letter of the correct form in the space above the adjective's number at the bottom of the page. You will need to divide the letters into words.

	Comparing Two Things	Comparing Three Things
1. short	T. shorter	C. shortiest
2. wet	M. weter	R. wettest
3. bright	D. brighter	L. brightliest
4. hungry	C. hungrier	R. hungryiest
5. wide	A. wider	E. wideest
6. happy	U. happyier	O. happiest
7. full	G. fuller	N. fullerist
8. narrow	N. narrower	T. narrowerest
9. pretty	D. prettyer	L. prettiest
10. strange	A. strangier	E. strangest
11. funny	K. funnyer	F. funniest

___ ___ ___ ___ ___ ___ ___ ___ ___ ___ ___ ___ ___ ___ ___
10 8   7   9   5   8   3   1   6   11 2   5   8   4   10

© Gary Robert Muschla

5.6 Calling Mr. President

Herbert Hoover was the first president to have one of these on his desk. What was it?

To answer the question, complete each sentence below with the correct adjective. Choose your answers from the words after each sentence. Write the letter of each answer in the space above its sentence number at the bottom of the page. You will need to divide the letters into words.

1. Julie's cell phone is _____ than Ali's cell phone.
   O. smaller   C. smallest

2. Ali's phone is _____ than Julie's.
   P. old   E. older

3. Ali's phone is also _____ than Julie's.
   A. heavier   E. heaviest

4. Bradley's phone is the _____ phone of all.
   R. better   H. best

5. His phone is the _____ phone of them all.
   G. newer   E. newest

6. The reception on Julie's phone is very _____.
   N. clear   O. clearer

7. Julie's phone is the _____ phone of all.
   N. thinner   L. thinnest

8. The battery in Julie's phone lasts _____.
   T. long   M. longer

9. Her phone is _____ to use than her brother's phone.
   P. easier   A. easiest

10. Julie feels that cell phones are the _____ invention ever.
    C. greater   E. greatest

___ ___ ___ ___ ___ ___ ___ ___ ___ ___
3   8   5   7   2   9   4   1   6   10

Adjectives

© Gary Robert Muschla

5.7 Manhattan

In 1626, Peter Minuit bought Manhattan from Native Americans. The name Manhattan comes from an Algonquian Indian term. What did this term mean?

To answer the question, read each sentence below. Decide if the underlined adjective is used correctly. If the form of the adjective is correct, write the letter for *correct* in the space above its sentence number at the bottom of the page. If it is incorrect, write the letter for *incorrect*. You will need to divide the letters into words.

1. To James, history is the <u>most interesting</u> subject in school.
   O. Correct   S. Incorrect

2. He likes learning about <u>brave</u> explorers.
   D. Correct   R. Incorrect

3. Some of the <u>greatest</u> explorers sailed to the New World.
   H. Correct   W. Incorrect

4. Some searched for the <u>most shortest</u> route to India.
   D. Correct   A. Incorrect

5. Others looked for <u>more greater</u> wealth.
   D. Correct   N. Incorrect

6. Some met the <u>baddest</u> of all misfortunes.
   P. Correct   F. Incorrect

7. Many explorers discovered <u>wonderful</u> lands.
   S. Correct   A. Incorrect

8. Settlements were built in the <u>most good</u> locations.
   L. Correct   I. Incorrect

9. Some settlements became <u>big</u> cities.
   L. Correct   N. Incorrect

<u> </u> <u> </u> <u> </u> <u> </u> <u> </u> <u> </u> <u> </u> <u> </u> <u> </u> <u> </u> <u> </u> <u> </u> <u> </u>
 8   7   9   4   5   2   1   6   3   8   9   9   7

© Gary Robert Muschla

Adjectives

5.8 Inventor of the Very First Computer

Many historians agree that the first computer was built in the seventeenth century. It was a mechanical adding machine. A French mathematician invented it. What was his name?

To answer the question, read each sentence below. Find the adjective. Only *one* adjective appears in each sentence. In the parentheses that follow each sentence, a letter is called for. Find this letter in the adjective. Then write the letter in the space above its sentence number at the bottom of the page. The first one is done for you.

1. <u>Basic</u> computers were built centuries ago. (fifth letter)

2. These machines could only add numbers. (fourth letter)

3. They were very simple. (fourth letter)

4. Several inventors worked on computers. (seventh letter)

5. Modern computers were developed in 1946. (fourth letter)

6. This computer was called ENIAC. (third letter)

7. ENIAC was extremely big. (first letter)

8. It weighed many tons. (second letter)

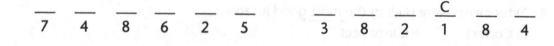

$$\overline{} \quad \overline{} \quad \overline{} \quad \overline{} \quad \overline{} \quad \overline{} \qquad \overline{} \quad \overline{} \quad \overline{} \quad \overset{C}{\overline{}} \quad \overline{} \quad \overline{}$$

7   4   8   6   2   5   3   8   2   1   8   4

Adjectives

© Gary Robert Muschla

5.9 Studying the Earth

Some scientists study the structure of the earth. What are these scientists called?

To answer the question, complete each sentence below with the correct adjective form. Choose your answers from the words after each sentence. Write the letter of each answer in the space above its sentence number at the bottom of the page.

1. Rashid's _____ brother studies the earth.
   A. old   O. older

2. He told Rashid many _____ facts.
   S. interesting   U. more interesting

3. The Pacific Ocean is the _____ ocean of all.
   S. largest   M. most largest

4. Mount Everest is _____ than any other mountain on earth.
   O. taller   T. more taller

5. The _____ mountain in North America is Mount McKinley.
   E. higher   I. highest

6. Greenland is the _____ island on our planet.
   R. bigger   L. biggest

7. Asia has the _____ population of any continent.
   D. greater   G. greatest

8. Antarctica has the _____ population of any continent.
   G. smallest   Y. most small

9. An atlas is a _____ book for learning about the earth.
   E. good   S. better

10. Rashid says his brother has the _____ job in the world.
    K. better   T. best

___ ___ ___ ___ ___ ___ ___ ___ ___ ___
 8   9   4   6   1   7   5   2   10   3

© Gary Robert Muschla

Adverbs

Adverbs are words that describe verbs, adjectives, and other adverbs. They most often modify verbs and tell *how*, *when*, *where*, *to what degree*, or *how often* the action of the verb is done. Many, but not all, adverbs end in *-ly*.

The tip sheets and worksheets that follow address various topics and skills related to adverbs. The first tip sheet and Worksheets 6.1 through 6.3 focus on identifying adverbs. The next tip sheet and Worksheets 6.4 through 6.6 focus on the comparison of adverbs. The final tip sheet and Worksheets 6.7 and 6.8 focus on double negatives, and Worksheets 6.9 through 6.11 offer reviews for adverbs.

Adverbs

• •

Adverbs are words that describe verbs, adjectives, or other adverbs.

- Adverbs usually answer one of the following questions in a sentence: *How? When? Where? How often?*

  Tom walked <u>quickly</u>. (how)

  He will go <u>later</u>. (when)

  Marie stood <u>there</u>. (where)

  She practices her flute <u>daily</u>. (how often)

- Many adverbs describe verbs. In each example below, *carefully* tells how Sue checked her math.

  <u>Carefully</u>, Sue checked her math.

  Sue <u>carefully</u> checked her math.

  Sue checked her math <u>carefully</u>.

- An adverb that describes an adjective or another adverb usually comes directly before the word it modifies.

  That tree is <u>very</u> tall. (adverb *very* modifying adjective *tall*)

  You must check your work <u>very</u> <u>carefully</u>. (adverb *very* modifying adverb *carefully*)

- Many, but not all, adverbs end in *-ly*. Following are some examples of common adverbs.

almost	completely	here	really	suddenly	very
always	deeply	loudly	recently	then	when
calmly	easily	often	so	there	where
clearly	happily	quickly	soon	totally	yet

• •

© Gary Robert Muschla

6.1 Bones of the Human Body

The average human baby is born with more than three hundred bones. As the baby gets older, some of the bones grow together. An adult has fewer bones than a baby. How many bones does the average human adult have?

To answer the question, find the adverb in each set of words below. Write the letter of the adverb in the space above its line number at the bottom of the page. You will need to divide the letters into words.

1. S. wonderful   N. quickly   R. eager   O. follow

2. U. rush   T. move   A. from   E. soon

3. T. finally   F. enjoy   N. movie   J. boat

4. R. river   D. ask   S. softly   M. sky

5. E. into   W. suddenly   F. picture   S. rainy

6. I. deeply   N. cold   L. hurry   R. short

7. T. walk   X. then   D. large   W. blue

8. L. ocean   E. tall   O. calmly   V. run

9. C. tell   T. careful   G. laughing   U. slowly

10. R. always   T. snowy   M. catch   U. look

11. B. question   U. do   N. end   H. happily

12. L. silent   P. entrance   D. where   I. step

___ ___ ___ ___ ___ ___ ___ ___ ___ ___ ___ ___ ___
3   5   8   11   9   1   12   10   2   12   4   6   7

© Gary Robert Muschla

Adverbs

6.2 Journey Westward

Many pioneers followed this route westward. What is the name of this route? To answer the question, read each sentence below. Find the adverb. Choose your answers from the underlined words. Write the letter of each answer in the space above its sentence number at the bottom of the page. You will need to divide the letters into words.

1. Sasha is almost done with her history report.
   E   R   W

2. Her topic about the pioneers is very interesting.
   H   N   V

3. Sasha studied her topic completely.
   M   W   A

4. She always checks the Internet for information.
   T   E   I

5. She quickly finds information on websites.
   G   C   I

6. She goes to the library and checks for information there.
   S   E   I

7. Sasha usually finds a lot of information.
   R   T   S

8. She writes her summary carefully.
   N   D   O

9. She will explain her project clearly.
   D   N   L

___ ___ ___ ___ ___ ___ ___ ___ ___ ___ ___
 8   7   1   5   8   2   4   7   3   6   9

© Gary Robert Muschla

Adverbs

6.3 Bats

Bats are mammals. They have a special ability that no other mammal has. What is this ability?

To answer the question, read the article below. Decide if the underlined words are adverbs. Start with the first sentence. Then write the letters beneath the adverbs in order in the spaces at the bottom of the page.

Many people <u>feel</u> that bats are <u>very</u> <u>scary</u> animals. Some people have <u>always</u>
　　　　　　　　　E　　　　　　　　　　F　　C　　　　　　　　　　　　　　　　　　L

been <u>afraid</u> of bats. But most bats are not a <u>threat</u> to people. In fact, they are <u>helpful</u>.
　　　　I　　　　　　　　　　　　　　　　　　　M　　　　　　　　　　　　　　　　R

Bats hunt at <u>night</u>. They streak <u>smoothly</u> and <u>silently</u> <u>through</u> the darkness in search of
　　　　　　　　I　　　　　　　　　Y　　　　　　　I　　　　　T

prey. <u>Most</u> bats eat insects. This <u>greatly</u> <u>reduces</u> the insect population. In the <u>early</u>
　　　　N　　　　　　　　　　　　　N　　　　　R　　　　　　　　　　　　　　　　　E

morning bats <u>finally</u> <u>return</u> to their roosts.
　　　　　　　　G　　　　　S

__   __   __   __   __   __

© Gary Robert Muschla

Comparing with Adverbs

Like adjectives, adverbs can be used to compare two or more things.

- To compare two things, add *-er* to most adverbs. To compare three or more things, add *-est*.

fast	faster	fastest
slow	slower	slowest

- For most adverbs of two or more syllables, use *more* or *most* for comparing.

quickly	more quickly	most quickly
suddenly	more suddenly	most suddenly

Here is an example of comparing with adverbs.

James came <u>early</u> to school.

Cory came <u>earlier</u> than James.

Vinny came <u>earliest</u> of all.

© Gary Robert Muschla

6.4 Fairy Tales

In the late 1600s, this French author wrote down many fairy tales. These stories had been told for generations. Two of the most famous are "Cinderella" and "Sleeping Beauty." What was this man's name?

To answer the question, find the correct adverb form. Choose the correct form from the words following the numbered adverb. Only one of the choices for each adverb will be correct. Write the letter of each answer in the space above the adverb's number at the bottom of the page.

	Comparing Two Things	**Comparing Three Things**
1. fast	I. more fast	T. fastest
2. early	P. earlier	E. most early
3. quickly	O. quicklier	H. most quickly
4. often	J. more oftener	U. most often
5. silently	S. more silently	R. silentliest
6. eagerly	E. more eagerly	O. eagerliest
7. near	A. nearer	R. most nearest
8. softly	M. softlier	L. most softly
9. gracefully	I. gracefullier	R. most gracefully
10. deeply	C. more deeply	N. deepliest

___ ___ ___ ___ ___ ___ ___   ___ ___ ___ ___ ___ ___ ___ ___
10   3   7   9   8   6   5   2   6   9   9   7   4   8   1

© Gary Robert Muschla

6.5 Standing Tall

In ancient Rome, giraffes were known by another name. What did the Romans call a giraffe?

To answer the question, complete each sentence below with the correct adverb form. Choose your answers from the words after each sentence. Write the letter of each answer in the space above its sentence number at the bottom of the page. You will need to divide the letters into words.

1. Africa is home to a _____ large number of animals.
   O. very   R. more very

2. Giraffes reach _____ into trees to eat leaves.
   R. high   N. more higher

3. Gazelles run _____ across the plains than other animals.
   N. gracefully   M. more gracefully

4. Ostriches run _____ than many four-legged animals.
   D. fast   P. faster

5. Of all the animals in Africa, which one runs _____?
   N. slow   D. slowest

6. Hippopotamuses rest _____ in the cool water of a river.
   A. lazily   O. more lazily

7. Scientists study the animals _____.
   C. patiently   L. more patiently

8. Some animals are studied _____ than others.
   E. easily   L. more easily

9. Of all animals, lions are studied _____ by scientists.
   G. more carefully   E. most carefully

___ ___ ___ ___ ___ ___ ___ ___ ___ ___ ___ ___
 7   6   3   9   8   8   9   1   4   6   2   5

© Gary Robert Muschla

Adverbs

6.6 By Another Name

This salamander is found in some rivers and lakes of the central and eastern United States. It has a very misleading name. What is its name?

To answer the question, read each sentence below. If the underlined adverb is used correctly, write the letter for *correct* in the space above its sentence number at the bottom of the page. If the adverb is used incorrectly, write the letter for *incorrect*. You will need to divide the letters into words.

1. Justin <u>clearly</u> is interested in animals.
   U. Correct   R. Incorrect

2. Of all the books he reads, he <u>most eagerly</u> reads books about animals.
   U. Correct   M. Incorrect

3. He finds animals to be <u>more very</u> interesting than any other subject.
   E. Correct   P. Incorrect

4. He reads every book about animals <u>most completely</u>.
   A. Correct   M. Incorrect

5. Justin <u>often</u> watches TV shows about animals.
   Y. Correct   S. Incorrect

6. Sometimes he stays up <u>later</u> at night to watch them.
   K. Correct   P. Incorrect

7. He <u>always</u> seems to be learning something new.
   P. Correct   A. Incorrect

8. He <u>greatly</u> enjoys learning about animals.
   D. Correct   P. Incorrect

$$\overline{\quad}\;\;\overline{\quad}\;\;\overline{\quad}\;\;\overline{\quad}\;\;\overline{\quad}\;\;\overline{\quad}\;\;\overline{\quad}\;\;\overline{\quad}$$
  4   2   8   7   1   6   3   5

© Gary Robert Muschla

Adverbs

Negative Words and Double Negatives

A *negative word* is a word that means "no." Some negative words are used as adverbs. Some negative words are contractions of verbs and the word *not*. The following are common negative words.

never	no	nobody	none
no one	not (-n't)	nothing	nowhere
aren't	can't	won't	isn't

- Use only one negative word in a sentence. Using two usually makes the sentence incorrect. Such a sentence is called a *double negative*.

    I have <u>no</u> pet. (correct)

    I do <u>not</u> have a pet. (correct)

    I do <u>not</u> have <u>no</u> pet. (double negative, incorrect)

- To correct a double negative, drop one of the negative words. You may also change one of the negative words to a positive word.

    I <u>don't</u> have <u>no</u> pencils. (double negative)

    I have <u>no</u> pencils. (correct)

    I <u>don't</u> have any pencils. (correct)

© Gary Robert Muschla

6.7 Dangerous Lizard

This poisonous lizard is found in the desert regions of the southwestern United States. What is its name?

To answer the question, find the negative word in each set of words below. Write the letter of each negative word in the space above its line number at the bottom of the page.

1. E. from   S. any   N. none   W. about

2. E. nothing   R. some   L. more   D. ever

3. O. own   I. does   A. haven't   S. than

4. C. every   M. not   E. something   P. anybody

5. V. low   G. often   I. goes   R. never

6. I. aren't   S. our   A. where   U. maybe

7. K. anything   B. might   S. nowhere   O. they

8. M. when   V. have   L. won't   J. your

9. R. then   A. are   O. seen   G. nobody

10. T. how   O. isn't   K. there   R. how

11. F. use   L. here   T. no   D. below

___ ___ ___ ___   ___ ___ ___ ___ ___ ___ ___
 9   6   8   3   4 10   1   7 11   2   5

© Gary Robert Muschla

Adverbs

6.8 Giant Storm

Many astronomers think that the biggest storm in our solar system is on Jupiter. What is this storm called?

    To answer the question, read each sentence below. If a sentence has only one negative word, write the letter for *correct* in the space above its number at the bottom of the page. If a sentence has two negative words, write the letter for *incorrect*. You will need to divide the letters into words.

1. Nobody doesn't know how big space is.
   U. Correct   D. Incorrect

2. Our solar system isn't the only solar system.
   S. Correct   N. Incorrect

3. Humans haven't explored very much of outer space.
   O. Correct   L. Incorrect

4. Some planets have many moons, and others have none.
   A. Correct   T. Incorrect

5. Mercury and Venus don't have no moons.
   O. Correct   E. Incorrect

6. These two planets do not have no life.
   E. Correct   P. Incorrect

7. Our moon has no atmosphere.
   H. Correct   T. Incorrect

8. It doesn't have no life either.
   A. Correct   R. Incorrect

9. No one knows if other planets have life.
   T. Correct   S. Incorrect

10. Astronauts haven't visited no other planets yet.
   R. Correct   G. Incorrect

___ ___ ___ ___ ___ ___ ___ ___ ___ ___ ___ ___ ___ ___ ___
9 7 5 10 8 5 4 9 8 5 1 2 6 3 9

Adverbs

© Gary Robert Muschla

6.9 Bacteria and Disease

This French scientist found that bacteria can cause disease. Who was he?

To answer the question, find the adverb in each sentence below. Only one adverb appears in each sentence. In the parentheses after each sentence, a letter is called for. Find this letter in the adverb. Then write the letter in the space above the sentence number at the bottom of the page. The first one is done for you.

1. Tia has <u>always</u> been interested in science. (first letter)

2. Recently her father bought her a microscope. (first letter)

3. Tia has wanted a microscope for a very long time. (second letter)

4. Curiously, she opened the box. (fourth letter)

5. She carefully put the microscope on the table. (sixth letter)

6. She would be looking at slides soon. (second letter)

7. She slowly put a slide under the microscope. (first letter)

8. Happily she looked at the slide. (third letter)

9. She could see bacteria clearly. (second letter)

10. She knew that she would use her microscope often. (third letter)

$$\overline{}_9 \; \overline{}_6 \; \overline{}_5 \; \overline{}_4 \; \overline{}_7 \quad \overline{}_8 \; \overline{\underset{1}{A}} \; \overline{}_7 \; \overline{}_{10} \; \overline{}_3 \; \overline{}_5 \; \overline{}_2$$

© Gary Robert Muschla

Adverbs

6.10 Start of a Star

Donald Duck first appeared in a cartoon in 1934. He soon went on to become a cartoon star. What was the name of this cartoon?

To answer the question, write the correct form of the adverb for comparing two or three things. After writing the correct form, find the letter called for in your answer. Write this letter in the space above the adverb's number at the bottom of the page. The first one is done for you. You will need to divide the letters into words.

1. easily   comparing two things ___more easily___ (seventh letter)

2. often   comparing three things _____ (ninth letter)

3. slowly   comparing three things _____ (eighth letter)

4. early   comparing two things _____ (fifth letter)

5. hard   comparing three things _____ (first letter)

6. fast   comparing three things _____ (seventh letter)

7. quickly   comparing two things _____ (tenth letter)

8. carefully   comparing two things _____ (fourth letter)

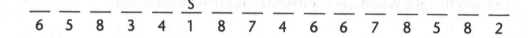

__ __ __ __ __ __S__ __ __ __ __ __ __ __ __ __
 6   5   8   3   4   1   8   7   4   6   6   7   8   5   8   2

Adverbs

© Gary Robert Muschla

6.11 Rescue Dogs

In the past, these dogs were trained to rescue people lost in the snow. It is believed that they saved thousands of lives. What is the name of this breed of dog?

To answer the question, read each sentence below. If the adverb is used correctly, write the letter for *correct* in the space above the sentence number at the bottom of the page. If an adverb is used incorrectly, write the letter for *incorrect*. You will need to divide the letters into words.

1. Dogs are clearly popular pets.
    E. Correct   I. Incorrect

2. Dogs more oftener become a "member" of the family.
    O. Correct   I. Incorrect

3. Some dogs bark more loudly than others.
    D. Correct   N. Incorrect

4. Greyhounds run fastest than most other dogs.
    M. Correct   T. Incorrect

5. A dog may act very bravely when protecting its owner.
    A. Correct   L. Incorrect

6. If you have patience, you will most easily train a dog.
    H. Correct   S. Incorrect

7. Dogs most usually become excited when visitors come.
    M. Correct   R. Incorrect

8. Puppies will chase a ball happily.
    N. Correct   T. Incorrect

9. Most dogs wait eagerly for their owners to come home.
    B. Correct   R. Incorrect

 __   __   __   __   __   __   __   __   __   __   __   __
  6   5   2   8   4   9   1   7   8   5   7   3

© Gary Robert Muschla

Adverbs

Prepositions, Conjunctions, and Interjections

The final three parts of speech are prepositions, conjunctions, and interjections. Each has a specific function in a sentence.

A *preposition* relates a noun or pronoun to another word in a sentence. All of the words related by a preposition, as well as the preposition itself, are a part of a prepositional phrase. The first two tip sheets and Worksheets 7.1 through 7.8 focus on prepositions, prepositional phrases, and objects of prepositions.

A *conjunction* is a word that joins words or groups of words in a sentence. One tip sheet and Worksheet 7.9 focus on *coordinating conjunctions*.

An *interjection* is a word that shows feeling or emotion. One tip sheet and Worksheet 7.10 focus on interjections.

Part 7 concludes with Worksheets 7.11 through 7.13, which review prepositions, conjunctions, and interjections, and Worksheet 7.14, which reviews parts of speech.

Prepositions

A *preposition* is a word that relates a noun or pronoun to another word in a sentence. The following are examples of common prepositions:

about	at	by	near	to
above	before	during	of	toward
across	behind	for	off	under
after	below	from	on	underneath
along	beside	in	out	with
among	between	inside	over	within
around	beyond	into	through	without

- The noun or pronoun that follows a preposition is called the *object of the preposition.*

  Sara likes reading about history.

  We walk to school.

  I had a lot of homework.

- Remember that only object pronouns can be used as objects of a preposition. The following are the object pronouns:

me	you	him	her	it	us	them

  The phone call was for me.

  I gave the book to her.

  The gift was from them.

© Gary Robert Muschla

7.1 A States

The names of these three states begin and end with the letter *A*. What states are they?

To answer the question, find the preposition in each set of words below. Write the letter of the preposition in the space above its line number at the bottom of the page. You will need to divide the letters into words.

1. E. real	R. very	S. through	N. your
2. O. into	N. are	E. me	I. always
3. V. finish	M. green	S. school	R. for
4. K. story	P. can	N. from	U. this
5. R. stars	K. at	W. and	C. best
6. O. does	M. someone	E. favorite	I. behind
7. L. along	J. guess	R. nowhere	O. today
8. S. is	H. walk	B. before	I. write
9. R. become	N. finally	F. he	Z. over
10. O. were	M. with	A. draw	T. race
11. N. other	E. come	U. often	A. beside

__ __ __ __ __ __ __ __ __ __ __ __ __ __ __ __ __ __ __ __
11 7 11 8 11 10 11 11 7 11 1 5 11 11 3 6 9 2 4 11

© Gary Robert Muschla

7.2 Insects

This insect has been bred for more than two thousand years. It is very important for making a certain kind of clothing. What is the name of this insect?

To answer the question, read the article below. Decide if the underlined words are prepositions. Start with the first sentence. Then write the letters beneath the prepositions in order in the spaces at the bottom of the page.

Insects <u>are</u> found <u>all</u> <u>around</u> the world. They live <u>in</u> forests, fields, <u>and</u> deserts.
P   L   S   I   R

They live <u>just</u> <u>about</u> everywhere. They are <u>even</u> <u>inside</u> your home. Some insects <u>are</u>
A   L   D   K   Y

destructive. They eat crops <u>and</u> cause damage <u>to</u> homes. Some cause disease. But others
M   W

are helpful. Honeybees <u>help</u> spread pollen <u>among</u> flowers. This <u>helps</u> the flowers bloom.
T   U   O   T

Other insects <u>eat</u> harmful bugs. Insects <u>are</u> an important <u>form</u> <u>of</u> life <u>on</u> <u>our</u> planet.
J   I   W R M S

___ ___ ___ ___ ___ ___ ___ ___ ___

© Gary Robert Muschla

7.3 Special Animals

Some mammals have flippers instead of feet. They belong to a special group of animals. What group of animals do these mammals belong to?

To answer the question, read each sentence below. Find the preposition. Choose your answers from the underlined words. Write the letter of each answer in the space above its sentence number at the bottom of the page.

1. Melissa went to the aquarium yesterday.
         A I   O

2. The aquarium was filled with people.
             U   E   W

3. She saw all kinds of sea animals.
       E A   I

4. She was amazed by the sharks.
       M   L   S

5. She laughed at the playful dolphins.
       E   N S

6. She watched them leap from the water.
           U   T   P

7. They would then dive deep below the surface.
            R   D N

8. Soon it was time for the show.
      S   J   P

9. Melissa's seat was near the pool.
        E   N A

___ ___ ___ ___ ___ ___ ___ ___ ___
8   3   9   5   1   6   2   7   4

© Gary Robert Muschla

Prepositional Phrases

A *prepositional phrase* includes a preposition, its object, and any words that describe the object.

- A prepositional phrase always starts with a preposition.

- A prepositional phrase always ends with a noun or pronoun. The noun or pronoun is the *object of the preposition*.

- Only object pronouns—*me, you, him, her, it, us, them*—can be the object in a prepositional phrase.

- Prepositional phrases can be at the beginning of a sentence, in the middle, or at the end. Here are some examples:

  Without my key, I couldn't get into the house.

  The roses in their yard are beautiful.

  We went to the mall yesterday.

  We rode in the new car.

  Maria was ill with a cold.

© Gary Robert Muschla

7.4 President's Plane

The president of the United States flies in a special jet. What is the name of the president's plane?

To answer the question, read each sentence below. Decide which under-lined words are prepositional phrases. Write the letter of each prepositional phrase in the space above its sentence number at the bottom of the page. You will need to divide the letters into words.

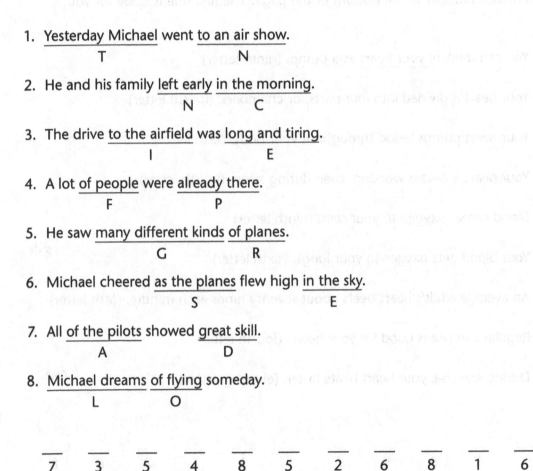

1. Yesterday Michael went to an air show.
        T   N

2. He and his family left early in the morning.
                N   C

3. The drive to the airfield was long and tiring.
          I   E

4. A lot of people were already there.
        F   P

5. He saw many different kinds of planes.
          G   R

6. Michael cheered as the planes flew high in the sky.
          S   E

7. All of the pilots showed great skill.
       A   D

8. Michael dreams of flying someday.
        L   O

$\overline{}\overline{}\overline{}\overline{}\overline{}\overline{}\overline{}\overline{}\overline{}\overline{}\overline{}$
 7   3   5   4   8   5   2   6   8   1   6

© Gary Robert Muschla

7.5 Body System

Your body has several systems. These systems are made up of organs that you need to live. One of these systems is made up of your heart, lungs, blood, and blood vessels. What is the name of this body system?

To answer the question, read each sentence below. Find the prepositional phrase. In the parentheses after each sentence, a letter is called for. Find the letter in the prepositional phrase, and write the letter in the space above its sentence number at the bottom of the page. The first one is done for you.

1. You can think <u>of your heart</u> as a pump. (ninth letter)

2. Your heart is divided into four parts, or chambers. (fourth letter)

3. Your heart pumps blood throughout your body. (fifth letter)

4. Your heart is always working, even during sleep. (fourth letter)

5. Blood carries oxygen to your cells. (ninth letter)

6. Your blood gets oxygen in your lungs. (sixth letter)

7. An average adult's heart beats about seventy times each minute. (fifth letter)

8. Regular exercise is good for your heart. (fourth letter)

9. During exercise, your heart beats faster. (eleventh letter)

$$\frac{\quad}{9} \quad \frac{\quad}{4} \quad \frac{\quad}{6} \quad \frac{\quad}{9} \quad \frac{\quad}{3} \quad \frac{\quad}{5} \quad \frac{A}{1} \quad \frac{\quad}{7} \quad \frac{\quad}{2} \quad \frac{\quad}{6} \quad \frac{\quad}{8}$$

© Gary Robert Muschla

7.6 Long Before E-Mail

Long ago, it might have taken weeks to send a letter from one part of the country to another. In the 1860s, riders on horses carried letters between St. Joseph, Missouri, and Sacramento, California. What was the name of this mail service?

To answer the question, read each sentence below. Find the object in the prepositional phrase. Choose your answers from the words after each sentence. Write the letter of each answer in the space above its sentence number at the bottom of the page. You will need to divide the letters into words.

1. Kevin would be lost without his computer.
   S. lost   X. computer

2. He uses his computer for school.
   E. computer   O. school

3. He researches topics on the Internet.
   N. topics   R. Internet

4. For entertainment, Kevin plays computer games.
   N. entertainment S. games

5. Each day he sends e-mail to his friends.
   R. e-mail   P. friends

6. In the evening he checks his messages.
   E. evening   P. messages

7. His friends send many messages to Kevin.
   E. messages   S. Kevin

8. In seconds he answers them.
   Y. seconds   T. them

___ ___ ___ ___ ___ ___ ___ ___ ___ ___ ___
 5   2   4   8   6   1   5   3   6   7   7

© Gary Robert Muschla

7.7 Soccer

This soccer tournament was first played in the country of Uruguay in 1930. What is the name of this soccer tournament?

To answer the question, read each sentence below. Find the object of the preposition. In the parentheses that follow each sentence, a letter is called for. Find this letter in the object of the preposition. Write the letter in the space above its sentence number at the bottom of the page. The first one is done for you. You will need to divide the letters into words.

1. Steve likes playing soccer with his <u>friends</u>. (second letter)

2. Sometimes they play after school. (fourth letter)

3. On Saturday they play too. (fourth letter)

4. If they have time, they will play on Sunday. (fourth letter)

5. During the week Steve finishes his homework first. (first letter)

6. Last summer Steve went to camp and played soccer. (first letter)

7. With practice, Steve will become a better player. (first letter)

8. The other members of his family enjoy soccer. (fifth letter)

$$\overline{}_{5} \quad \overline{}_{2} \quad \overset{R}{\overline{}}_{1} \quad \overline{}_{8} \quad \overline{}_{4} \quad \overline{}_{6} \quad \overline{}_{3} \quad \overline{}_{7}$$

© Gary Robert Muschla

7.8 Miniature Golf

Miniature golf was first played in this country in 1867. What country was this?

To answer the question, complete each sentence with the correct object pronoun. Choose your answers from the words after each sentence. Write the letter of each answer in the space above its sentence number at the bottom of the page.

1. Playing miniature golf is fun for Jessica and _____.
   E. I   T. me

2. Her brother spoke to _____ about the history of the game.
   A. us   U. we

3. The information was interesting to _____.
   O. I   C. me

4. It was interesting to _____, too.
   S. she   D. her

5. We met some friends and played miniature golf with _____.
   O. them   L. they

6. "I will keep score for _____," I said.
   P. we   S. us

7. I told Jessica that I had a golf club for _____.
   N. her   C. she

8. I told her brother that I also had a club for _____.
   Y. he   L. him

__	__	__	__	__	__	__	__
6	3	5	1	8	2	7	4

© Gary Robert Muschla

Conjunctions

Conjunctions are words that join words or groups of words in a sentence. They can also join two sentences to form a compound sentence. Three of the most common conjunctions are *and*, *but*, and *or*.

- Use *and* to join words, groups of words, or sentences.

  Sean <u>and</u> Pete are friends.

  Cori <u>and</u> her sister are twins.

  Kristen finished her homework, <u>and</u> she went to dance practice.

- Use *but* to join two sentences that show contrast.

  I hoped for snow, <u>but</u> it rained.

  Heather wanted to watch TV, <u>but</u> she had too much homework.

- Use *or* to join words or sentences that show choice.

  Ricky <u>or</u> Sam will be the starting pitcher.

  Jasmine will practice her flute, <u>or</u> she will read her novel.

© Gary Robert Muschla

7.9 One of the Very First Cars

In 1885, Karl Benz of Germany test-drove a gas-powered vehicle. It had only three wheels, but many historians consider it to be one of the first cars. What was it called?

   To answer the question, complete each sentence with the correct conjunction. Choose your answers from the words after each sentence. Write the letter of each answer in the space above its sentence number at the bottom of the page.

1. Karl Benz _____ Henry Ford were inventors of automobiles.
   A. and   E. or

2. Benz worked in Germany, _____ Ford worked in the United States.
   E. but   U. or

3. Inventors in England _____ France also built early automobiles.
   N. but   R. and

4. Many men tried to build automobiles, _____ not all were successful.
   L. and   T. but

5. Ford built his first car in 1893, _____ Benz tested his many years earlier.
   N. but   S. and

6. These early machines were often called "horseless carriages," _____ they had other names, too.
   R. or   W. but

7. In time, the new machines were called automobiles _____ cars.
   V. but   M. or

8. My mother _____ father have their own cars.
   G. and   J. or

9. My father drives either his car _____ his truck to work each day.
   O. or   K. and

| — | — | — | — | — | — | — | — | — | — |
| 7 | 9 | 4 | 9 | 3 | 6 | 1 | 8 | 2 | 5 |

© Gary Robert Muschla

Interjections

An *interjection* is a word or group of words that expresses strong feeling. The following list contains common interjections.

aha	hey	oh, dear	phew
gee	hooray	oh, no	ugh
good grief	my goodness	oops	wow
great	oh	ouch	well

- An interjection that expresses strong feeling is followed by an exclamation point. Such interjections stand alone, either before or after a sentence.

  <u>Oh, no!</u> I forgot to do my homework.

  <u>Wow!</u> What a catch.

  I got an A on my test. <u>Phew!</u>

- An interjection that expresses a milder feeling usually appears at the beginning of a sentence. It is followed by a comma.

  <u>Oh,</u> that's how you got the answer.

  <u>Gee,</u> I never thought of that.

© Gary Robert Muschla

7.10 Ancient Astronomer

People once believed that the earth was the center of the universe. This ancient Greek was one of the first people to believe that the earth traveled around the sun. Who was he?

To answer the question, find the interjection in each sentence below. In the parentheses after each sentence, a letter is called for. Find this letter in the interjection. Then write the letter in the space above its sentence number at the bottom of the page. The first one is done for you.

1. <u>He</u>y, my class is learning about the solar system. (first letter)

2. We are going on a class trip to a planetarium. Great! (fifth letter)

3. The buses are here. Terrific! (fifth letter)

4. Watch out! Always look before crossing the street to get on a bus. (fourth letter)

5. Ugh! I have to sit in the front seat. (first letter)

6. Oops, I think I left my lunch at home. (fourth letter)

7. Aha, here it is in the bottom of my knapsack. (first letter)

8. Good grief, the ride to the planetarium is taking forever. (sixth letter)

								H		
7	8	3	6	2	7	8	4	1	5	6

© Gary Robert Muschla

7.11 Puzzling Pastime

In 1760, Englishman John Spilsbury invented this enjoyable amusement. It is still popular today. What did Spilsbury invent?

To answer the question, match the word or words with their most accurate label. Write the letter of each answer in the space above its line number at the bottom of the page. If the given labels do not apply, write the letter for *neither*. You will need to divide the letters into words.

1. of   E. Conjunction   A. Preposition   O. Neither

2. oh no   S. Prepositional Phrase   U. Interjection   I. Neither

3. are   U. Conjunction   L. Preposition   I. Neither

4. after school   E. Prepositional Phrase   A. Interjection   Y. Neither

5. for   D. Conjunction   S. Preposition   N. Neither

6. but   L. Conjunction   R. Preposition   V. Neither

7. my goodness   T. Prepositional Phrase   P. Interjection   K. Neither

8. soon   V. Conjunction   C. Preposition   G. Neither

9. the house   A. Prepositional Phrase   M. Interjection   Z. Neither

10. or   W. Conjunction   R. Preposition   N. Neither

11. by the pond   Q. Preposition   J. Prepositional Phrase   S. Neither

12. and   Z. Conjunction   H. Preposition   N. Neither

___   ___   ___   ___   ___   ___   ___   ___   ___   ___   ___   ___
11   3   8   5   1   10   7   2   12   9   6   4

© Gary Robert Muschla

7.12 Studying Bugs

This scientist studies insects. What is this scientist called?

To answer the question, read each sentence below. Decide if all of the underlined words make up prepositional phrases. If all of the underlined words make up prepositional phrases, write the letter for *correct* in the space above their sentence number at the bottom of the page. If any underlined words in the sentence are not a part of a prepositional phrase, write the letter for *incorrect*.

1. Tyler often looks for bugs with his father.
   M. Correct   U. Incorrect

2. His father is a scientist who studies insects.
   T. Correct   N. Incorrect

3. Tyler knows many different kinds of insects.
   R. Correct   I. Incorrect

4. Insects are found in most parts of the world.
   L. Correct   N. Incorrect

5. Insects live on land and also in water.
   E. Correct   I. Incorrect

6. Many people are afraid of insects.
   G. Correct   I. Incorrect

7. Some insects, such as mosquitoes, cause disease.
   N. Correct   S. Incorrect

8. Bees help spread pollen among flowers.
   T. Correct   C. Incorrect

9. Tyler thinks studying insects is a lot of fun.
   H. Correct   O. Incorrect

___ ___ ___ ___ ___ ___ ___ ___ ___ ___ ___ ___
 5   2   8   9   1   9   4   9   6   3   7   8

© Gary Robert Muschla

7.13 Lots of Animals

This is the largest of all animal groups. It includes insects, arachnids (spiders), and crustaceans (shrimp and lobsters). What is the name of this animal group?

To answer the question, read each sentence below. Decide if the sentence has a prepositional phrase. If it does, find the object of the preposition. Choose your answers from the words after each sentence. Write the letter of each answer in the space above its sentence number at the bottom of the page. If a sentence has no prepositional phrase, write the letter for *none*.

1. There are many different kinds of animals.
   M. kinds   H. animals   C. none

2. Animals are found all around the world.
   H. all   P. world   R. none

3. Some animals are very small, and others are very big.
   T. small   N. others   S. none

4. Fish are animals that breathe with gills.
   W. animals   T. gills   I. none

5. They live in water and have scales.
   D. water   R. scales   N. none

6. Birds have feathers and fly with wings.
   E. feathers   A. wings   O. none

7. Mammals are an important animal group.
   S. animal   C. group   R. none

8. A few mammals hatch from eggs, but most are born live.
   O. eggs   U. live   E. none

___ ___ ___ ___ ___ ___ ___ ___ ___ ___
6   7   4   1   7   8   2   8   5   3

© Gary Robert Muschla

7.14 Ski Tournament

In 1892, the first international ski tournament was held in a Scandinavian country. The tournament took place near a city called Christiania. Today that city has a different name. What is the name of this city today? In what country is it located?

To answer the question, read each sentence below. Name the part of speech of the underlined word. Choose your answers from the parts of speech after the sentences. Write the letter of each answer in the space above its sentence number at the bottom of the page. You will need to divide the letters into words.

1. Stacey <u>lives</u> in New England.

2. Her <u>town</u> receives a lot of snow each winter.

3. She <u>and</u> her friends like to ski.

4. <u>They</u> wait for the first snowfall each season.

5. Stacey bought <u>new</u> skis this year.

6. She loves skiing <u>swiftly</u> down the mountain.

7. "<u>Great!</u> It's going to snow," Stacey said.

8. The next morning she looked outside <u>at</u> the deep snow.

Answers

L. Noun   R. Verb   A. Adjective   N. Conjunction
W. Preposition   S. Pronoun   Y. Adverb   O. Interjection

__	__	__	__	__	__	__	__	__	__
7	4	2	7	3	7	1	8	5	6

© Gary Robert Muschla

Punctuation and Capitalization

Understanding punctuation and capitalization is important to understanding grammar. Punctuation and capitalization help make writing clear. Imagine a paragraph composed of sentences with no punctuation marks or capital letters. Such a paragraph would be a challenge to read.

The tip sheets and worksheets that follow concentrate on punctuation and capitalization. The first tip sheet and Worksheets 8.1 and 8.2 address abbreviations. The next six tip sheets and Worksheets 8.3 through 8.18 focus on punctuation—end marks, commas, colons, hyphens, apostrophes, quotation marks, and italics—while Worksheets 8.19 through 8.28 offer general reviews of punctuation. The final tip sheet and Worksheets 8.29 through 8.33 focus on capitalization, with Worksheet 8.34 providing a review of capitalization.

Abbreviations

Abbreviations are shortened forms of words. Many abbreviations start with a capital letter and end with a period. A list of common abbreviations follows.

Days of the Week

Sun.	Sunday
Mon.	Monday
Tues.	Tuesday
Wed.	Wednesday
Thurs.	Thursday
Fri.	Friday
Sat.	Saturday

Months

Jan.	January	Aug.	August
Feb.	February	Sept.	September
Mar.	March	Oct.	October
Apr.	April	Nov.	November
Jun.	June	Dec.	December
Jul.	July		

Streets

St.	Street
Rd.	Road
Ave.	Avenue
Blvd.	Boulevard
Dr.	Drive

Titles

Mr.	Mister	Pres.	President
Mrs.	Mistress	Capt.	Captain
Dr.	Doctor	Sr.	Senior
Gov.	Governor	Jr.	Junior

Businesses

Co.	Company
Corp.	Corporation
Inc.	Incorporated

Time

A.M. or a.m.	before noon
P.M. or p.m.	after noon

© Gary Robert Muschla

8.1 More Common than You May Think

About 45,000 of these occur each day around the world. What are they?

To answer the question, match each word with its abbreviation. Write the letter of each answer in the space above its number at the bottom of the page.

1. Street   C. Str.   R. St.

2. Doctor   R. Doc.   N. Dr.

3. Saturday   O. Sat.   A. Sa.

4. Company   H. Co.   O. Comp.

5. January   I. J.   E. Jan.

6. Avenue   U. Ave.   R. Av.

7. Wednesday   M. Wed.   E. Wedn.

8. August   N. Augt.   R. Aug.

9. Senior   A. Sn.   D. Sr.

10. Corporation   P. Cor.   S. Corp.

11. December   T. Dec.   H. De.

$\overline{\hspace{1em}}$ $\overline{\hspace{1em}}$ $\overline{\hspace{1em}}$ $\overline{\hspace{1em}}$ $\overline{\hspace{1em}}$ $\overline{\hspace{1em}}$ $\overline{\hspace{1em}}$ $\overline{\hspace{1em}}$ $\overline{\hspace{1em}}$ $\overline{\hspace{1em}}$ $\overline{\hspace{1em}}$ $\overline{\hspace{1em}}$ $\overline{\hspace{1em}}$

11   4   6   2   9   5   1   10   11   3   8   7   10

© Gary Robert Muschla

8.2 Born in the U.S.A.

This president was the first U.S. president to be born a U.S. citizen. All of the presidents before him were born citizens of England. Who was he?

To answer the question, write the full word that makes up each abbreviation. In the parentheses after each term, a letter is called for. Find this letter in your answer. Then write it in the space above the abbreviation's number at the bottom of the page. The first one is done for you. You will need to divide the letters into words.

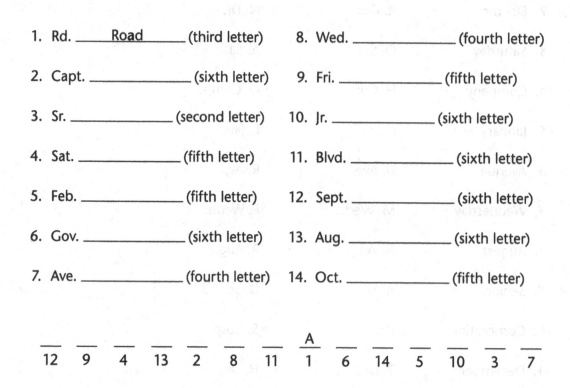

1. Rd. _____Road_____ (third letter)

2. Capt. _____ (sixth letter)

3. Sr. _____ (second letter)

4. Sat. _____ (fifth letter)

5. Feb. _____ (fifth letter)

6. Gov. _____ (sixth letter)

7. Ave. _____ (fourth letter)

8. Wed. _____ (fourth letter)

9. Fri. _____ (fifth letter)

10. Jr. _____ (sixth letter)

11. Blvd. _____ (sixth letter)

12. Sept. _____ (sixth letter)

13. Aug. _____ (sixth letter)

14. Oct. _____ (fifth letter)

__	__	__	__	__	__	__	A	__	__	__	__	__	__
12	9	4	13	2	8	11	1	6	14	5	10	3	7

© Gary Robert Muschla

End Punctuation

. . . .

End punctuation includes periods, question marks, and exclamation points. Use end punctuation to end a sentence.

- A period ends a statement or command.

  It is a sunny day.

  We will go to the movies tonight.

  Please open the window.

- A question mark ends a question.

  Will it snow tonight?

  Do we have homework?

  What is our math homework?

- An exclamation point ends an exclamation.

  Look out!

  Oh, no! I left my report home.

  What a catch! Wow!

- Use a period in most abbreviations and after initials.
  Mr.   Mrs.   Dr.   Ave.   St.   Capt.
  J. K. Rowling   John F. Kennedy   E. B. White

© Gary Robert Muschla

8.3 Bachelor President

This U.S. president was the only president never to have been married. Who was he?

To answer the question, read each sentence below. Choose the correct end punctuation. Write the letter of each answer in the space above its sentence number at the bottom of the page. You will need to divide the letters into words.

1. Luis and his friends are learning about the presidents
   U. Period   E. Question Mark   S. Exclamation Point

2. George Washington was the first president of the United States
   H. Period   P. Question Mark   C. Exclamation Point

3. Do you know who was the second
   F. Period   **J. Question Mark**   W. Exclamation Point

4. Abraham Lincoln was the president during the Civil War
   C. Period   I. Question Mark   R. Exclamation Point

5. He was also the tallest president
   E. Period   M. Question Mark   A. Exclamation Point

6. How tall was he
   M. Period   **B. Question Mark**   H. Exclamation Point

7. Franklin Roosevelt was elected for four straight terms
   M. Period   T. Question Mark   K. Exclamation Point

8. That's amazing
   G. Period   R. Question Mark   **N. Exclamation Point**

9. Bill Clinton was the first left-handed president
   S. Period   U. Question Mark   R. Exclamation Point

10. Who do you think will be the next president
    E. Period   **A. Question Mark**   I. Exclamation Point

J A M E S   B U C H A N A N
3 10 7   5   9   6   1   4   2   10 8   10   8

Punctuation and Capitalization

168

© Gary Robert Muschla

8.4 Stargazer

This American astronomer studied stars and galaxies. He found that the universe is filled with galaxies. A famous telescope is named in honor of him. Who was he?

To answer the question, read each sentence below. If the end punctuation is correct, write the letter for *correct* in the space above the sentence number at the bottom of the page. If the end punctuation is incorrect, write the letter for *incorrect*. You will need to divide the letters into words.

1. The sun is at the center of our solar system.
   - (N. Correct)   W. Incorrect

2. The planets travel around the sun.
   - (U. Correct)   A. Incorrect

3. How many planets are in our solar system!
   - J. Correct   (W. Incorrect)

4. Our solar system is a part of a galaxy.
   - (L. Correct)   R. Incorrect

5. I wonder what the name of our galaxy is?
   - S. Correct   (I. Incorrect)

6. Please check its name in that science book?
   - G. Correct   (E. Incorrect)

7. Isn't it called the Milky Way!
   - A. Correct   (D. Incorrect)

8. It contains about two hundred billion stars.
   - (H. Correct)   M. Incorrect

9. Wow. That's an incredible number.
   - L. Correct   (B. Incorrect)

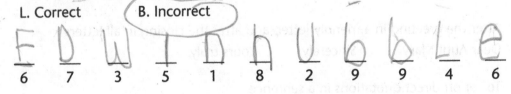

E D W I D h U b b L e
6   7   3   5   1   8   2   9   9   4   6

© Gary Robert Muschla

Punctuation and Capitalization

TIP SHEET

Commas

Commas have many uses in sentences. Use a comma for the following:

- To separate the words in a series

  Laurie had math, science, and history for homework.

- Before the conjunctions *and, but,* and *or* when forming a compound sentence

  Casey wanted to play baseball, but his brother wanted to play soccer.

- To set off introductory words and phrases

  No, the team hasn't scored yet.

  Scared by the thunder, the puppy hid behind the couch.

- To set off appositives (An appositive is a group of words that tells about a noun.)

  Kimberly, John's younger sister, was always causing mischief.

  Mrs. Williams, our principal, is always smiling.

  The snowstorm, the first of the season, made driving dangerous.

- To set off nouns in direct address

  Danny, it's time to leave.

  The book is on the desk, Tierra.

  I told you, Carly, we have to be home by two.

- Between the name of a city or town and its state

  Miami, Florida   Los Angeles, California   Chicago, Illinois

- Between the day and year in a date

  September 1, 2010   December 31, 2010

- After the greeting in a friendly letter, and after the closing in all letters

  Dear Aunt Mary,   Sincerely,   Yours truly,

- To set off direct quotations in a sentence

  "The movie begins at seven," said Ashley.

  Geena said, "I hope the sun comes out."

  "After I get home," said Tom, "I'll start my science project."

© Gary Robert Muschla

8.5 Big Boulder

This granite boulder in Wyoming covers about twenty-seven acres. Some five thousand names of pioneers are carved on it. What is the name of this boulder?

To answer the question, read each sentence below. If the commas in the sentence are used correctly, write the letter for *correct* in the space above the sentence number at the bottom of the page. If a comma in the sentence is missing or is used incorrectly, write the letter for *incorrect*. You will need to divide the letters into words.

1. Angelina, her little brother, and her parents went on a vacation.
   R. Correct   O. Incorrect

2. They went, to Yellowstone National Park in Wyoming.
   E. Correct   I. Incorrect

3. They left from Chicago, Illinois, and they drove to Yellowstone.
   W. Correct   H. Incorrect

4. Angelina enjoyed the drive, but her brother didn't.
   F. Correct   L. Incorrect

5. "Angelina there it is," said her brother as they neared the park.
   O. Correct   G. Incorrect

6. Angelina, and her brother soon learned many things about the park.
   L. Correct   D. Incorrect

7. Yellowstone, the first national park in the United States, is known for its great beauty.
   T. Correct   F. Incorrect

8. The park was established on March 1, 1872.
   S. Correct   E. Incorrect

9. It is a wonderful park, and the family enjoyed their visit.
   R. Correct   T. Incorrect

10. Someday they might go to California, or they might go to Florida.
    E. Correct   H. Incorrect

R E O I S T E R O E t h e d e s e r t

 9 10 5   2   8   7 10 9   1   4   7   3 10   6 10   8 10   9   7

© Gary Robert Muschla

8.6 First Settlement

The Spanish built this settlement in 1565. It became the first permanent European settlement in what was to become the United States. Today it is a city. What is its name?

To answer the question, read each sentence below. If the end punctuation and commas are used correctly, write the letter for *correct* in the space above the sentence number at the bottom of the page. If punctuation is missing or is used incorrectly, write the letter for *incorrect*. You will need to divide the letters into words.

1. The English Spanish French and Dutch all claimed parts of the New World.
   T. Correct   G. Incorrect

2. Life was hard in the New World, and some of the first settlements failed.
   I. Correct   M. Incorrect

3. Do you know what the first English settlement was.
   C. Correct   T. Incorrect

4. I'm not sure if it was Jamestown?
   N. Correct   E. Incorrect

5. The *Mayflower*, a small ship brought the Pilgrims to the New World.
   R. Correct   A. Incorrect

6. Did the Pilgrims settle in Massachusetts, or did they settle in New York?
   S. Correct   J. Incorrect

7. They reached the New World on Nov, 21 1620.
   M. Correct   U. Incorrect

8. The Pilgrims built the first permanent English settlement in Massachusetts.
   N. Correct   E. Incorrect

S A I N T A U G U S T I N E
6 5 2 8 3 5 7 1 7 6 3 2 8 4

© Gary Robert Muschla

8.7 Mighty River

This is the longest river in the world. It is 4,160 miles long. What is its name? On what continent is it found?

To answer the questions, read each sentence below. Decide if the end marks and commas are used correctly. If an end mark is missing or is used incorrectly, write the letter for *end mark* in the space above the sentence number at the bottom of the page. If a comma is missing or is used incorrectly, write the letter for *comma*. If the sentence is correct, write the letter for *no mistake*. You will need to divide the letters into words.

1. Most rivers empty into other rivers, lakes, or oceans.
   S. End Mark   E. Comma   G. No Mistake

2. Some rivers are thousands of miles long, but others are only a few miles.
   N. End Mark   R. Comma   A. No Mistake

3. Many rivers are more than a thousand miles long.
   D. End Mark   C. Comma   R. No Mistake

4. What is the longest river in the world.
   L. End Mark   W. Comma   O. No Mistake

5. The Mississippi River is the longest river in the United States.
   U. End Mark   A. Comma   F. No Mistake

6. The Amazon River, the second longest river in the world, is in South America.
   T. End Mark   R. Comma   N. No Mistake

7. The place where a river begins is called its source.
   A. End Mark   R. Comma   N. No Mistake

8. A river always flows downhill to its mouth.
   G. End Mark   U. Comma   I. No Mistake

N , L L e A E R I C a
6   8 4 1 7 5 2 8 3 7

© Gary Robert Muschla

Punctuation and Capitalization

173

Colons and Hyphens

Colons and hyphens have special uses. Use a colon for the following:

- To set off words in a list

  Brianna wrote down supplies she needed for school: pencils, pens, paper, and notebooks.

- Between hours and minutes in time

  10:30 A.M.   9:45 P.M.

- After the greeting of a business letter

  Dear Ms. Hernandez: Dear Mr. Smith:

  Use a hyphen for the following:

- To form certain compound words

  able-bodied   brother-in-law   self-made   stand-in

- To break words into syllables

  far-ther   nar-row   out-side   riv-er

© Gary Robert Muschla

8.8 Leaky Faucet

A faucet in Jason's house leaks at a rate of one drop of water each minute. This adds up to a lot of water. About how many gallons of water would Jason's leaky faucet waste in one year?

To answer the question, read each sentence below. Decide if the colons and hyphens are used correctly. If a colon is missing or is used incorrectly, write the letter for *colon* in the space above the sentence number at the bottom of the page. If a hyphen is missing or is used incorrectly, write the letter for *hyphen*. If the sentence is correct, write the letter for *no mistake*. You will need to reverse and divide the letters into words.

1. At 9,30 A.M. on Saturday, Jason helped his father fix a leaky faucet.
   U. Colon   E. Hyphen   A. No Mistake

2. Jason got the following tools for his father: a wrench, a screwdriver, and a flashlight.
   N. Colon   T. Hyphen   E. No Mistake

3. First they turned the water-off under the sink.
   A. Colon   I. Hyphen   O. No Mistake

4. Next: Jason's father loosened the faucet.
   H. Colon   R. Hyphen   T. No Mistake

5. Carefully his father took the faucet off: and he checked it.
   R. Colon   A. Hyphen   S. No Mistake

6. It was an oldfashioned faucet and had to be replaced.
   M. Colon   D. Hyphen   S. No Mistake

7. Jason's father had a new faucet, and by 9:55 the job was done.
   F. Colon   T. Hyphen   N. No Mistake

___	___	___	___	___	___	___	___	___	___	___
6	2	5	6	7	1	4	2	7	3	7

© Gary Robert Muschla

Apostrophes

Apostrophes are used to show the possessive case of nouns. They are also used to show where letters have been left out in contractions. Use an apostrophe to:

- Show the possessive case of singular nouns by adding an apostrophe and -s

  Vicky's room   James's coat   the rabbit's hole

  the baby's playpen   the school's playground   the tree's branches

- Show the possessive case of plural nouns that end in -s by adding an apostrophe

  the two sisters' room   the puppies' bed   the boys' soccer team

- Show the possessive case of plural nouns that do not end in -s by adding an apostrophe and -s

  a women's clothing store   the children's bikes   the oxen's plow

- Show the letters that are left out in a contraction

  I am—I'm   cannot—can't   do not—don't   could have—could've

  they are—they're   that is—that's   you will—you'll   it is—it's

© Gary Robert Muschla

8.9 Famous Artist

This woman is one of Mexico's most famous artists. What is her name?

To answer the question, match the words on the left with their correct form on the right. Choose your answers according to the form called for in the parentheses after the word. Write the letter of each answer in the space above its line number at the bottom of the page.

1. boy (plural possessive)   A. boys'   I. boy's

2. tree (singular possessive)   T. trees'   A. tree's

3. cat (plural possessive)   U. cat's   I. cats'

4. town (singular possessive)   H. town's   N. towns'

5. child (plural possessive)   I. childrens'   D. children's

6. father (singular possessive)   E. fathers'   O. father's

7. girl (singular possessive)   R. girl's   O. girls'

8. mouse (plural possessive)   L. mices'   F. mice's

9. cannot (contraction)   K. can't   V. cann't

10. we have (contraction)   R. w've   L. we've

$\overline{}$ $\overline{}$ $\overline{}$ $\overline{}$ $\overline{}$ $\overline{}$ $\overline{}$ $\overline{}$ $\overline{}$ $\overline{}$
   8   7   3   5   2   9   1   4   10   6

© Gary Robert Muschla

Punctuation and Capitalization

177

8.10 End of the Revolutionary War

The last major battle of the Revolutionary War was fought in Virginia. At what place was this battle fought?

To answer the question, read each sentence below. If the apostrophes are used correctly, write the letter for *correct* in the space above the sentence number at the bottom of the page. If an apostrophe is used incorrectly or is missing, write the letter for *incorrect*. You will need to reverse the letters.

1. British troops' fought American patriots' in the Revolutionary War.
   W. Correct   R. Incorrect

2. The Americans' fought bravely for independence.
   K. Correct   N. Incorrect

3. England's king didn't expect the colonists to rebel.
   O. Correct   E. Incorrect

4. The colonies' leaders signed the Declaration of Independence.
   K. Correct   N. Incorrect

5. George Washington was the colonial army's general.
   T. Correct   Y. Incorrect

6. The British couldn't destroy the patriots desire for liberty.
   E. Correct   O. Incorrect

7. The war lasted for many year's.
   N. Correct   Y. Incorrect

8. The war's last major battle was fought in Virginia in 1781.
   W. Correct   R. Incorrect

$\overline{}$ $\overline{}$ $\overline{}$ $\overline{}$ $\overline{}$ $\overline{}$ $\overline{}$ $\overline{}$
 2   8   6   5   4   1   3   7

© Gary Robert Muschla

8.11 First Vice President

Just about every American knows that George Washington was our country's first president. Who was the first vice president of the United States?

To answer the question, read the paragraph below. Decide if each underlined apostrophe is used correctly. Start with the first sentence. Then write the letters beneath the correctly used apostrophes in order in the spaces at the bottom of the page. You will need to divide the letters into words.

Billy's Aunt Jane is an expert on the president's. There aren't many thing's Aunt
    J   A   O   M

Jane doesn't know about our nation's leaders'. She knows all of the presidents' name's,
    H   N   E   A   S

their birthdays', and their home state's. She knows the years' of each man's presidency.
    M   U   G   D

Aunt Jane wrote books' about the presidents'. Billy's favorite is about George
                  R   E   A

Washington. The book tells about Washington's youth. Aunt Jane believes George
                                  M

Washington was one of our country's greatest president's.
                            S   E

__ __ __ __ __ __ __ __ __

© Gary Robert Muschla

Quotation Marks

Quotation marks are used to set off the words of speakers and to show certain titles.

- Use quotation marks to set off the direct words of a speaker. A direct quote begins with a capital letter. It is usually separated from the rest of the sentence by a comma. Sometimes a quotation ends with a question mark or exclamation point. Commas and end marks are placed inside the quotation marks.

  "It is a nice day," said Lindsay.

  Anthony said, "The game starts at eight."

  "When is our book report due?" asked Rebecca.

- Sometimes the direct words of a speaker are divided by the speaker's name. Use commas to separate the speaker from his or her direct words. If the second part of the quotation starts a new sentence, it must begin with a capital letter.

  "On Saturday," said Allie, "we can go shopping."

  "It is supposed to rain Saturday," she said. "Let's go shopping."

- Use quotation marks to show the titles of short stories, songs, articles, chapters of books, and poems.

  Story: "The Magic Carpet"

  Song: "America the Beautiful"

  Article: "How to Survive Fifth Grade"

  Chapter of book: "Babysitting Tips for Kids"

  Poem: "Alligator on the Escalator"

© Gary Robert Muschla

8.12 Meteors

Meteoroids are rocks that enter the earth's atmosphere from outer space. They usually burn up in the atmosphere. As they burn, they leave a streak of light. This streak of light is called a meteor. Many people mistakenly use another name for a meteor. What is this common name for a meteor?

To answer the question, read each sentence below. Decide if the sentence contains a direct quotation and needs quotation marks. If the sentence needs quotation marks, write the letter for *yes* in the space above its number at the bottom of the page. If the sentence does not need quotation marks, write the letter for *no*. You will need to divide the letters into words.

1. I like learning about outer space said Natalie.
   I. Yes   E. No

2. Me too said Michelle, her friend.
   A. Yes   U. No

3. The girls were studying outer space in their science class.
   S. Yes   H. No

4. Mrs. Thompson, their teacher, made the class interesting.
   N. Yes   G. No

5. Mrs. Thompson told the students to open their books.
   E. Yes   T. No

6. You are to read about meteors she said.
   N. Yes   H. No

7. Does anyone know what a meteor is? she asked.
   R. Yes   D. No

8. Natalie raised her hand.
   E. Yes   O. No

9. Yes, Natalie, said Mrs. Thompson, calling on her.
   S. Yes   A. No

___ ___ ___ ___ ___ ___ ___ ___ ___ ___ ___ ___
9   3   8   8   5   1   6   4   9   5   2   7

© Gary Robert Muschla

8.13 Volcanoes and Earthquakes

Many volcanoes and earthquakes occur around the Pacific Ocean. What is the special name for all of these volcanoes and earthquakes?

To answer the question, read each sentence below. If the quotation marks and the punctuation with them are correct, write the letter for *correct* in the space above the sentence number at the bottom of the page. If the quotation marks or punctuation with them is incorrect, write the letter for *incorrect*. You will need to divide the letters into words.

Punctuation and Capitalization

1. "Volcanoes and earthquakes cause much destruction, said Mrs. Jones."
    L. Correct   F. Incorrect

2. Mrs. Jones told her students to read Chapter 4, "The Violent Earth."
    F. Correct   H. Incorrect

3. "I like learning about volcanoes and earthquakes," Geraldo said.
    I. Correct   E. Incorrect

4. Geraldo recently watched a "TV special" about volcanoes.
    T. Correct   E. Incorrect

5. "I watched that show, too, said Madison. It was interesting."
    L. Correct   N. Incorrect

6. Victor told Mrs. Jones that he read an article titled "The Shaking Earth."
    I. Correct   A. Incorrect

7. "It was about earthquakes, he said.
    S. Correct   G. Incorrect

8. "A big earthquake can destroy a whole city," Geraldo said.
    R. Correct   A. Incorrect

9. "That's what happened in San Francisco in 1906," said Mrs. Jones.
    R. Correct   M. Incorrect

10. "I would never want to be near an earthquake or volcano" said Madison.
    E. Correct   O. Incorrect

$\overline{}$ $\overline{}$ $\overline{}$ $\overline{}$ $\overline{}$ $\overline{}$ $\overline{}$ $\overline{}$ $\overline{}$ $\overline{}$
 9   3   5   7   10   1   2   6   8   4

© Gary Robert Muschla

8.14 Landlocked

Only two countries of South America are landlocked. This means that they are surrounded by the land of other countries. One of these landlocked countries is Bolivia. What is the other?

To answer the question, read each sentence below. If the quotation marks and the punctuation with them are correct, write the letter for *correct* in the space above the sentence number at the bottom of the page. If the quotation marks or punctuation with them is incorrect, write the letter for *incorrect*.

1. "I'm going to do my social studies report on Bolivia," said Elena.
   A. Correct   U. Incorrect

2. "That's where my grandfather grew up," she said.
   A. Correct   I. Incorrect

3. "Isn't Bolivia in South America," said Marc.
   R. Correct   A. Incorrect

4. "Yes, said Elena, near Brazil."
   G. Correct   R. Incorrect

5. "Have you chosen a topic for your report?" Elena asked.
   Y. Correct   A. Incorrect

6. "Yes" said Marc. "My topic is the Panama Canal."
   E. Correct   U. Incorrect

7. He showed her a magazine article titled The Canal.
   A. Correct   P. Incorrect

8. "There's a lot of information in this article," he said.
   G. Correct   N. Incorrect

___ ___ ___ ___ ___ ___ ___ ___
 7   3   4   1   8   6   2   5

© Gary Robert Muschla

Italics

· ·

Italics are used to show certain titles and names. They are also used to highlight words. Italics are letters that lean to the right in printed material. In handwritten material, underlining is used in place of italics.

Use italics (or underlining) to show the following:

- The titles of books, movies, and TV shows

  Book: *Where the Red Fern Grows*

  Movie: *The Incredibles*

  TV show: *The Simpsons*

- The names of newspapers and magazines

  Newspaper: *New York Times*

  Magazine: *Cricket*

- Highlighting of words

  It's and *its* do not mean the same thing.

© Gary Robert Muschla

8.15 First Female Police Officer

In 1910, this woman became a police officer for the Los Angeles Police Department. She was the first female police officer in the nation with the power to arrest lawbreakers. What was her name?

To answer the question, decide if the names and titles below need italics. If a name or title is correctly written in italics, write the letter for *correct* in the space above its number at the bottom of the page. If a name or title is incorrect, write the letter for *incorrect*. You will need to divide the letters into words.

1. *Sunset Avenue* (street)   R. Correct   E. Incorrect

2. *Dallas Cowboys* (football team) I. Correct   E. Incorrect

3. *New York Times* (newspaper) I. Correct   R. Incorrect

4. *Training Your Pet* (book)   L. Correct   H. Incorrect

5. *America the Beautiful* (song) M. Correct   A. Incorrect

6. *Sesame Street* (TV show)   S. Correct   H. Incorrect

7. *Lassie* (movie)   L. Correct   A. Incorrect

8. *Island of the Blue Dolphins* (novel) L. Correct   T. Incorrect

9. *The Milky Way* (our galaxy) O. Correct   C. Incorrect

10. *Rocky Mountains* (mountain chain) P. Correct   W. Incorrect

__	__	__	__	__	__	__	__	__	__
5	7	3	9	1	10	2	8	4	6

© Gary Robert Muschla

8.16 Discoverer of Bacteria

In 1674, Dutchman Anton van Leeuwenhoek used a simple microscope and discovered bacteria. What did Leeuwenhoek call bacteria?

To answer the question, read each sentence below. If the underlined words should be italicized, write the letter for *italics* in the space above the sentence number at the bottom of the page. If the underlined words should not be italicized, write the letter for *no italics*.

1. Allan has always been interested in <u>science</u>.
   C. Italics   U. No Italics

2. Allan's father bought a <u>microscope</u> for him.
   R. Italics   M. No Italics

3. His father gave Allan a book titled <u>How to Use a Microscope</u>.
   S. Italics   Y. No Italics

4. Allan's microscope is different than the one <u>Leeuwenhoek</u> used.
   S. Italics   C. No Italics

5. Allan's father read an article about bacteria in a magazine called <u>Science</u>.
   N. Italics   H. No Italics

6. He also read about bacteria in the <u>New York Times</u>.
   E. Italics   V. No Italics

7. Leeuwenhoek was an excellent <u>scientist</u>.
   U. Italics   I. No Italics

8. Allan is planning to read a book about <u>the life of Anton van Leeuwenhoek</u>.
   M. Italics   A. No Italics

9. Tonight Allan will watch a TV show titled <u>Great Scientists of the Past</u>.
   L. Italics   E. No Italics

___ ___ ___ ___ ___ ___ ___ ___ ___ ___ ___
8   5   7   2   8   9   4   1   9   6   3

Punctuation and Capitalization

© Gary Robert Muschla

8.17 Ellis Island First

In 1892, this woman from Ireland became the first immigrant to pass through Ellis Island. What was her name?

To answer the question, decide if each name or title on the left requires quotation marks or italics. Choose your answers from the column labeled "Quotation Marks" or the column labeled "Italics." Write the letter of each answer in the space above its number at the bottom of the page. You will need to divide the letters into words.

	Quotation Marks	Italics
1. Pocahontas (movie)	S	M
2. The Star-Spangled Banner (song)	I	U
3. The Race (short story)	O	C
4. All About the Weather (book)	S	N
5. Studying for Tests (book chapter)	E	H
6. The Los Angeles Times (newspaper)	M	O
7. Maniac Magee (novel)	U	N
8. Wind (poem)	R	U
9. Sesame Street (TV show)	S	A
10. The Art of Skateboarding (article)	E	N

___ ___ ___ ___ ___ ___ ___ ___ ___ ___
9   7   4   2   10   1   6   3   8   5

© Gary Robert Muschla

8.18 Speedy Dog

This breed of dog is considered to be the fastest runner of all dogs. What dog is this?

To answer the question, read each sentence below. Decide if the underlined word or words need quotation marks or italics. Write the letter of each answer in the space above its sentence number at the bottom of the page. If neither quotation marks nor italics are needed, write the letter for *neither*. You will need to reverse the letters.

Punctuation and Capitalization

1. Kayla read a book titled Caring for Your Dog.
   L. Quotation Marks   E. Italics   I. Neither

2. In Chapter 2, Training Your Puppy, she learned many helpful tips.
   O. Quotation Marks   U. Italics   E. Neither

3. She learned that puppies need a lot of care.
   D. Quotation Marks   T. Italics   Y. Neither

4. Her mom handed her a magazine for dog owners.
   I. Quotation Marks   U. Italics   N. Neither

5. The name of the magazine was Dogs.
   O. Quotation Marks   R. Italics   U. Neither

6. You may find more information here, her mom said.
   U. Quotation Marks   I. Italics   C. Neither

7. Kayla turned to an article titled Your Dog and You.
   G. Quotation Marks   M. Italics   R. Neither

8. Maybe we can find more information on the Internet, said her mom.
   D. Quotation Marks   R. Italics   L. Neither

9. Of course, Kayla's favorite movie is 101 Dalmatians.
   F. Quotation Marks   H. Italics   R. Neither

$\overline{}$ $\overline{}$ $\overline{}$ $\overline{}$ $\overline{}$ $\overline{}$ $\overline{}$ $\overline{}$ $\overline{}$
  8   4   6   2   9   3   1   5   7

© Gary Robert Muschla

8.19 Measuring the Power of Earthquakes

Earthquakes can cause great destruction. In 1935, this man created a way to measure the power of an earthquake. Who was he?

To answer the question, match the phrase describing the use of a punctuation mark on the left with its name on the right. Write the letter of each answer in the space above the phrase's number at the bottom of the page.

1. separates words in a series

A. period

2. shows the title of a book

C. question mark

3. ends a declarative sentence

R. exclamation point

4. is used to show time

S. comma

5. shows a speaker's direct words

I. colon

6. shows ownership

H. hyphen

7. ends an interrogative sentence

E. quotation marks

8. is used with some compound words

T. italics

9. ends a sentence of strong feeling

L. apostrophe

7	8	3	9	6	5	1		9	4	7	8	2	5	9

© Gary Robert Muschla

8.20 Explorer of Florida

In the early 1520s, Juan Ponce de León explored Florida. Legend says that he searched for a fantastic spring. He believed that waters from this spring could keep a person young forever. What was this spring called?

   To answer the question, read each sentence below and find the missing punctuation mark. Choose your answers from the choices after each sentence. Write the letter of each answer in the space above its sentence number at the bottom of the page. You will need to divide the letters into words.

Punctuation and Capitalization

1. Nathans favorite subject in school is history.
   W. Comma   E. Period   I. Apostrophe

2. He enjoys reading about explorers and their discoveries
   A. Comma   U. Period   H. Apostrophe

3. "What is your favorite subject" he asked William.
   S. Comma   A. Question Mark   H. Apostrophe

4. "I really like science" said William.
   Y. Comma   F. Period   E. Apostrophe

5. Tamara said that her favorite subject is reading
   T. Comma   M. Quotation Marks   H. Period

6. "Whats your favorite book?" asked William.
   O. Comma   S. Quotation Marks   N. Apostrophe

7. She told him that the title of the book was Where the Red Fern Grows.
   E. Comma   H. Quotation Marks   T. Italics

8. "I read that book, Nathan said, in fifth grade."
   E. Comma   F. Quotation Marks   R. Colon

9. "It was a great book," he said "but my favorite books are about history."
   O. Comma   I. Quotation Marks   S. Italics

___ ___ ___ ___ ___ ___ ___ ___ ___ ___ ___ ___ ___ ___ ___
 8   9   2   6   7   3   1   6   9   8   4   9   2   7   5

© Gary Robert Muschla

8.21 Is There a Doctor in the House?

This doctor specializes in taking care of children. What kind of doctor is this?
To answer the question, read each sentence below and find the missing punctuation mark. Choose your answers from the choices after each sentence. Write the letter of each answer in the space above its sentence number at the bottom of the page.

1. Amy's mom took her to the doctor
   L. Comma   R. Period   D. Apostrophe

2. They arrived at the office at 230 P.M.
   M. Comma   H. Period   C. Colon

3. Dr. Williams took Amys temperature.
   U. Comma   N. Period   T. Apostrophe

4. "A hundred and two, she said.
   T. Comma   E. Italics   N. Quotation Marks

5. "Does your throat hurt" Dr. Williams asked.
   I. Comma   E. Period   A. Question Mark

6. Amy tried to answer but she could barely speak.
   D. Comma   S. Period   T. Quotation Marks

7. Amy was sick for the next few days with a terrible cold
   R. Comma   E. Period   A. Hyphen

8. She read a novel titled A Wrinkle in Time.
   E. Comma   P. Italics   O. Quotation Marks

9. "Hurray" she said excitedly when she was able to return to school.
   S. Comma   U. Period   I. Exclamation Point

___ ___ ___ ___ ___ ___ ___ ___ ___ ___ ___ ___
8   7   6   9   5   3   1   9   2   9   5   4

© Gary Robert Muschla

8.22 Constellation

This constellation is easy to see. Two of its stars point to the North Star. What is the common name of this constellation?

To answer the question, read each sentence below and find the missing punctuation mark. Choose your answers from the choices after each sentence. Write the letter of each answer in the space above its sentence number at the bottom of the page. You will need to reverse and divide the letters into words.

1. Toby his brother, and father went to a space museum.
   I. Comma   A. Period   O. Apostrophe

2. They woke up early and left at 8:00 AM
   H. Comma   E. Period   M. Colon

3. The drive was long and they didn't arrive until ten.
   I. Comma   U. Colon   E. Apostrophe

4. They visited all of the exhibits
   T. Comma   R. Period   N. Colon

5. "Which one did you like the best?" Tobys father asked.
   D. Comma   J. Period   P. Apostrophe

6. "I liked the one about the stars, Toby said.
   W. Comma   T. Period   G. Quotation Marks

7. "No I liked the one about the moon," said his brother.
   D. Comma   I. Period   T. Quotation Marks

8. "Did you like the show in the planetarium" their father asked.
   L. Period   S. Comma   B. Question Mark

9. They stayed at the museum until 500 P.M.
   U. Comma   E. Period   P. Colon

___   ___   ___   ___   ___   ___   ___   ___   ___
4   2   9   5   1   7   6   3   8

© Gary Robert Muschla

Punctuation and Capitalization

8.23 Much Bigger than a Mouse

The biggest rodent in the world is found in South America. It can grow to be four feet long and weigh up to a hundred pounds. What is it called?

To answer the question, read each sentence below and find the missing punctuation mark. Choose your answers from the choices after each sentence. Write the letter of each answer in the space above its sentence number at the bottom of the page.

1. One of Emily's favorite books is Stuart Little.
   R. Apostrophe   M. Quotation Marks   B. Italics

2. "Mice are rodents, she said to her friend Richard.
   I. Apostrophe   A. Quotation Marks   E. Italics

3. "They are warmblooded animals," she said.
   U. Comma   Y. Period   A. Hyphen

4. There are almost five thousand different kinds of rodents
   N. Comma   Y. Period   S. Quotation Marks

5. Richards pet guinea pig is a rodent.
   R. Comma   A. Apostrophe   B. Colon

6. Most rodents are small but some are big.
   C. Comma   L. Period   H. Apostrophe

7. "I think," said Richard "that the biggest rodent lives in South America."
   R. Comma   E. Period   O. Apostrophe

8. "Do you know its name" said Emily.
   T. Apostrophe   P. Question Mark   G. Comma

$$\overline{}\quad\overline{}\quad\overline{}\quad\overline{}\quad\overline{}\quad\overline{}\quad\overline{}\quad\overline{}$$
  6   2   8   4   1   3   7   5

© Gary Robert Muschla

8.24 Minus Snakes

Punctuation and Capitalization

This is the only major land mass in the world where there are no snakes. What is it?

To answer the question, read each sentence below and find the missing punctuation mark. Choose your answers from the choices listed after the sentences. Write the letter of each answer in the space above its sentence number at the bottom of the page. Not all of the answers will be used. Some of the answers will be used more than once.

1. Snakes are reptiles and they frighten many people.

2. Snakes are coldblooded creatures.

3. A snakes body is covered with scales.

4. "Do you know how many kinds of snakes there are" asked Melissa.

5. There are about twenty-five hundred, said Harrison.

6. "I never knew there were so many" said Melissa.

7. "Snakes are found in most parts of the world, said Harrison

8. "Theres a show about snakes on TV tonight," he said.

9. "A good book to read is Snakes Around the World," Harrison said.

10. I don't like snakes," said Melissa.

Answers

A. Quotation Marks   N. Question Mark   T. Comma   E. Colon   I. Italics

M. Exclamation Point   R. Hyphen   C. Apostrophe   O. Period

___ ___ ___ ___ ___ ___ ___ ___ ___ ___
10   4   6   7   2   8   1   9   3   5

© Gary Robert Muschla

8.25 American Legend

According to legend, Pecos Bill was the greatest American cowboy. His horse was as tough as he was. What was the name of Pecos Bill's horse?

To answer the question, read each sentence below and find the missing punctuation mark. Choose your answers from the choices listed after the sentences. If no punctuation mark is missing, write the letter for *none*. Write the letter of each answer in the space above its sentence number at the bottom of the page. Not all of the answers will be used.

1. Wesleys class is reading tall tales.

2. The stories about Pecos Bill are very popular.

3. Bill is the greatest cowboy in history and he performed super feats.

4. Wesley's alltime favorite story is the one where Bill lassoes a tornado.

5. "Wow" said Nicole with great surprise. "I like that one, too."

6. "I like the stories of Paul Bunyan better, said Thomas.

7. "You can find more of these stories in a book called American Tall Tales," she said.

8. "Is it in the library" asked Wesley.

9. "Yes," she said, "but the library closes today at 315."

Answers
T. Period   M. Question Mark   O. Comma   W. Colon   K. Italics

I. None   D. Exclamation Point   E. Hyphen   A. Apostrophe   R. Quotation Mark

___ ___ ___ ___ ___ - ___ ___ ___ ___ ___
9   2   5   3   9   8   1   7   4   6

© Gary Robert Muschla

8.26 Down by the Sea

Lobsters, crabs, and shrimp belong to this class of animals. What is this class of animals called?

To answer the question, read each sentence below. If all the punctuation is correct, write the letter for *correct* in the space above the sentence number at the bottom of the page. If any of the punctuation is incorrect, write the letter for *incorrect*.

1. Billy's father is the captain of a fishing boat.
   E. Correct   O. Incorrect

2. His fathers boat has two crewmen.
   G. Correct   U. Incorrect

3. Most mornings the men leave the dock by 6-00 A.M.
   N. Correct   T. Incorrect

4. Fishing is hard work, and they dont return until late in the evening.
   E. Correct   N. Incorrect

5. They are always watchful for storms.
   R. Correct   C. Incorrect

6. Rough seas force them back to port early.
   S. Correct   M. Incorrect

7. Hurricanes, the most powerful ocean storms are a threat during the summer and fall.
   U. Correct   A. Incorrect

8. Billy loves the sea, and he wants to have his own boat someday.
   C. Correct   N. Incorrect

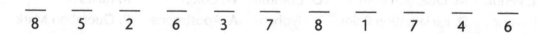

__ __ __ __ __ __ __ __ __ __ __
8   5   2   6   3   7   8   1   7   4   6

© Gary Robert Muschla

8.27 Turning from Side to Side

This is the only insect that can turn its head from side to side. What is it?

To answer the question, read each sentence below. If all the punctuation is correct, write the letter for *correct* in the space above the sentence number at the bottom of the page. If any of the punctuation is incorrect, write the letter for *incorrect*.

1. I don't like bugs, said Hannah.
   S. Correct   M. Incorrect

2. "Me neither" said Jill. "I never did."
   D. Correct   T. Incorrect

3. "Some insects are important," said Brandon.
   R. Correct   H. Incorrect

4. "What kind of bug is important," said Hannah.
   O. Correct   G. Incorrect

5. "Ladybugs," said Brandon, "They eat other bugs."
   N. Correct   S. Incorrect

6. "And bees," he said, "because they help to spread pollen on flowers."
   Y. Correct   A. Incorrect

7. Brandon was the bug expert in his class.
   A. Correct   I. Incorrect

8. "You should read a book about *insects*," he said.
   E. Correct   N. Incorrect

9. "I read *Charlotte's Web* for my book report," said Hannah.
   P. Correct   D. Incorrect

10. "That's about a spider," said Brandon, "and spiders are arachnids."
    I. Correct   E. Incorrect

___ ___ ___ ___ ___ ___ ___   ___ ___ ___ ___ ___ ___
 9   3   7   6   10 8   4   1   7   8   2   10 5

© Gary Robert Muschla

8.28 American Royalty

This is the only place in the United States that has a royal palace. Where is it?

To answer the question, read each sentence below. If all the punctuation is correct, write the letter for *correct* in the space above the sentence number at the bottom of the page. If any of the punctuation is incorrect, write the letter for *incorrect*.

1. "In the past, said Mr. Ortiz, kings ruled many countries."
   E. Correct   O. Incorrect

2. "Has the United States ever had a king," he asked the class?
   I. Correct   O. Incorrect

3. Ariel knew the answer, and she quickly raised her hand.
   U. Correct   A. Incorrect

4. "No," she said when Mr Ortiz called on her.
   U. Correct   O. Incorrect

5. "Thats right," he said. "The king of England was the king of the thirteen colonies."
   R. Correct   L. Incorrect

6. "Some kings were wise rulers," he said "but others were mean."
   R. Correct   N. Incorrect

7. Mr. Ortiz assigned the homework.
   L. Correct   N. Incorrect

8. Students had to read Chapter 7, *Our First President*, in their books.
   M. Correct   H. Incorrect

___ ___ ___ ___ ___ ___ ___ ___
 8   2   6   1   5   4   7   3

© Gary Robert Muschla

Capitalization

Always capitalize the following:

- The pronoun *I*

- Proper nouns

  George Washington   Judy Blume   Golden Gate Bridge

- Proper adjectives

  American students   Mexican food   the French people

- Initials

  John F. Kennedy   J. K. Rowling   E. B. White

- Titles when they come before a name

  Doctor Smith   Captain Hernandez   Aunt Janet   Pastor Jackson

- The days of the week and the months of the year

  Sunday   Monday   Wednesday   Saturday

  January   April   August   November

- The names of cities, states, countries, and continents

  New York   Colorado   United States of America   Africa

- The names of rivers, lakes, oceans, mountains, and other geographical sites

  Rio Grande River   Lake Superior   Pacific Ocean   Mount Everest

  Rocky Mountains   Sahara Desert   Grand Canyon   North Pole

- The names of streets and avenues

  Main Street   Sunrise Court   River Avenue   Hillside Road

- The names of public and religious holidays

  Fourth of July   Christmas   Yom Kippur   Ramadan

- The names of companies, organizations, agencies, and clubs

  Ford Motor Company   Federal Bureau of Investigation

  the Smithton Better Business Bureau   the Pleasantville Ice Skating Association

(continued)

© Gary Robert Muschla

Capitalization (continued)

- The first word in a sentence

  Snow fell through the night.

- The first word in a quotation

  Sharon said, "The book report is due Friday."

- The first word, last word, and all important words in the titles of books, poems, songs, movies, TV shows, and plays

  Book: *Bridge to Terabithia*

  Poem: "A Patch of Old Snow"

  Song: "America the Beautiful"

  Movie: *101 Dalmatians*

  TV show: *The Simpsons*

  Play: *Beauty and the Beast*

- All of the words of the greeting of a letter (Only capitalize the first word of the closing of a letter.)

  Dear Uncle Jim,   Sincerely yours,   Yours very truly,

- Most abbreviations

  Mr.   Mrs.   Dr.   Ave.   Tues.   Dec.

© Gary Robert Muschla

8.29 Butterfly by Another Name

Butterflies were not always called butterflies. What was an earlier name for a butterfly?

To answer the question, find the correct capitalization for each item below. Write the letter of each answer in the space above its number at the bottom of the page.

1. uncle bill
   F. uncle Bill   R. Uncle Bill

2. lincoln memorial
   A. Lincoln memorial   U. Lincoln Memorial

3. mrs. williams
   T. Mrs. Williams   M. mrs. Williams

4. sunrise street
   E. Sunrise street   Y. Sunrise Street

5. captain smith
   L. Captain Smith   P. captain Smith

6. *a wrinkle in time* (novel)
   B. *A Wrinkle in Time*   R. *a Wrinkle in Time*

7. rio grande river
   J. Rio Grande river   T. Rio Grande River

8. dr. alice e. walton
   M. Dr. Alice e. Walton   F. Dr. Alice E. Walton

9. "how to train a puppy" (article)
   E. "How to Train a Puppy"   O. "How To Train A Puppy"

___ ___ ___ ___ ___ ___ ___ ___ ___
 8   5   2   7   3   9   1   6   4

© Gary Robert Muschla

8.30 South Pacific Explorer

This English explorer discovered the eastern coast of Australia. He explored many of the islands of the South Pacific Ocean. He also was the first to cross the Antarctic Circle. Who was he?

To answer the question, decide which letter in each of the following is incorrect. This may be a letter that needs to be capitalized, or it may be a letter that is capitalized but should not be. Write the letter in the space above its number at the bottom of the page. You will need to divide the letters into words.

1. Jason's Sister

2. Dr. David o. Williams

3. Hamilton Hiking club

4. a Jellyfish

5. ken's Mower Shop

6. an Elephant

7. Big Pond avenue

8. mr. Thomas

9. United States Of America

___ ___ ___ ___ ___ ___ ___ ___ ___
 4   7   8   6   1   3   9   2   5

© Gary Robert Muschla

8.31 Flowing Backward

On December 16, 1811, parts of the Mississippi River flowed backward. What caused this?

To answer the question, find the correctly capitalized term or phrase in each pair. Write the letter of each answer in the space above its line number at the bottom of the page.

1. U. Rocky Mountains   E. Atlantic ocean

2. C. Maple street   T. Mrs. Helen Brown

3. R. the Month of January   H. Gulf of Mexico

4. E. Johnny's Pizza Shop   O. woofer, our dog

5. R. los Angeles   A. Missouri River

6. O. oceans of the World   A. E. B. White

7. K. Mount McKinley   D. dr. Peterson

8. Q. Great Plains   L. Alaska, a State

9. G. captain Martin   E. the continent of North America

10. R. Tues., Nov. 10th   E. new Jersey

___ ___ ___ ___ ___ ___ ___ ___ ___ ___
9   5   10   2   3   8   1   6   7   4

Punctuation and Capitalization

© Gary Robert Muschla

8.32 Heading to Brazil

Punctuation and Capitalization

In 1500, this Portuguese explorer set out to sail around Africa to India. But strong winds and ocean currents pushed him off course. He eventually discovered Brazil. Who was he?

To answer the question, read each sentence below. If all of the capital letters are correct, write the letter for *correct* in the space above the sentence number at the bottom of the page. If a letter that should be capitalized is not capitalized, or if a letter that should not be capitalized is capitalized, write the letter for *incorrect*.

1. After Columbus discovered the new World, European explorers sailed westward.
   H. Correct   B. Incorrect

2. Spanish and Portuguese explorers sought Routes to Asia.
   A. Correct   E. Incorrect

3. Some of these men explored South America.
   L. Correct   U. Incorrect

4. Others sailed around Africa to India.
   O. Correct   E. Incorrect

5. The French and English explored much of North America.
   C. Correct   M. Incorrect

6. Sailing across the Atlantic ocean was long and dangerous.
   A. Correct   D. Incorrect

7. Strong winds and powerful storms forced ships off course.
   A. Correct   H. Incorrect

8. Many ships were lost in Hurricanes.
   G. Correct   P. Incorrect

9. Settlers came after the explorers and started Colonies.
   J. Correct   R. Incorrect

___ ___ ___ ___ ___   ___ ___ ___ ___ ___ ___
 8   2   6   9   4   5   7   1   9   7   3

© Gary Robert Muschla

8.33 Peninsula State

A peninsula is land surrounded on three sides by water. Which state is made of two major peninsulas?

To answer the question, read each sentence below. If all of the capital letters are correct, write the letter for *correct* in the space above the sentence number at the bottom of the page. If a letter that should be capitalized is not capitalized, or if a letter that should not be capitalized is capitalized, write the letter for *incorrect*.

1. Olivia is the geography Expert in Mrs. Martino's class.
   R. Correct   H. Incorrect

2. "Is Fargo the capital of North Dakota?" asked Robert.
   A. Correct   L. Incorrect

3. "No," Olivia said. "it's Bismarck."
   A. Correct   I. Incorrect

4. "What's the biggest State?" another student asked.
   E. Correct   I. Incorrect

5. "Alaska," said Olivia, "and the next biggest is Texas."
   C. Correct   O. Incorrect

6. "Which of the Great Lakes is the biggest?" asked Michael.
   N. Correct   A. Incorrect

7. "Lake Superior," Olivia said. "The smallest is lake Ontario."
   F. Correct   M. Incorrect

8. Olivia was able to answer everyone's questions about the Geography of the United States that day.
   R. Correct   G. Incorrect

__	__	__	__	__	__	__	__
7	3	5	1	4	8	2	6

© Gary Robert Muschla

8.34 Lands Down Under

Geographers give Australia, New Zealand, and many of the Pacific Islands a special name. Together, what are these places called?

To answer the question, read each sentence below. Find the incorrect letter. This letter may be a letter that needs to be capitalized, or it may be a letter that is capitalized but should not be. Write the letter in the space above its sentence number at the bottom of the page.

1. The world is divided into seven Continents.

2. The biggest one in the world is asia.

3. Africa is the second largest, and north America is the third.

4. Do you know what Ocean is the biggest?

5. it is the Pacific Ocean, which is twice as big as the Atlantic.

6. The Equator divides the world into a northern half and a southern half.

7. The United States of america stretches from the Atlantic Ocean to the Pacific Ocean.

$$\overline{}\quad\overline{}\quad\overline{}\quad\overline{}\quad\overline{}\quad\overline{}\quad\overline{}$$
4   1   6   2   3   5   7

© Gary Robert Muschla

Usage and Proofreading

Word usage is an important part of grammar. Words like *accept* and *except*, *good* and *well*, and *lay* and *lie* are easy to mix up. Even if you understand the meanings of these words, you may make mistakes with them if you are not careful. Because these words, and words like them, are easily confused, they may slip into your speaking and writing. You can avoid making usage mistakes by (1) understanding the meanings of easily confused words, and (2) proofreading your written work with care.

The tip sheets and worksheets that follow focus on word usage and proofreading. The first tip sheet identifies several of the most easily confused words, and Worksheets 9.1 through 9.4 provide practice in recognizing and using these words correctly. The next tip sheet offers guidelines for proofreading for grammar mistakes, and Worksheets 9.5 through 9.14 focus on proofreading practice, which provides a general review of grammar.

Confusing Words

Some words in English are easily confused. They result in many mistakes for speakers and writers. The following list contains some of the most common of these words.

- accept—except

  accept (verb)—to receive or to agree to

  except (preposition)—not including; leaving out; but

- all ready—already

  all ready (adjective)—completely prepared

  already (adverb)—by this time

- breath—breathe

  breath (noun)—air inhaled and exhaled

  breathe (verb)—to inhale and exhale air

- council—counsel

  council (noun)—an official group

  counsel (verb)—to offer advice

  counsel (noun)—advice

- country—county

  country (noun)—a nation

  county (noun)—a part of a state in the United States

- dairy—diary

  dairy (noun)—a place where milk is produced or stored

  diary (noun)—a personal journal

- desert—dessert

  desert (noun)—very dry land

  dessert (noun)—food served at the end of a meal

(continued)

© Gary Robert Muschla

Confusing Words (continued)

- its—it's

  its (pronoun)—possessive form of *it*

  it's (contraction)—*it is*

- later—latter

  later (adverb)—after a certain time

  latter (adjective)—the second of two

- lay—lie

  lay (verb)—to set or place something down

  lie (verb)—to recline or to rest

- loose—lose

  loose (adjective)—not tight

  lose (verb)—misplace; not win

- picture—pitcher

  picture (noun)—a drawing or photograph

  pitcher (noun)—a container for holding a liquid; a baseball player

- quiet—quit—quite

  quiet (adjective)—little or no noise

  quit (verb)—to stop

  quite (adverb)—very

- their—there—they're

  their (pronoun)—possessive case of *they*

  there (adverb)—in, at, or near a particular place

  they're (contraction)—*they are*

(continued)

© Gary Robert Muschla

Confusing Words (continued)

- threw—through

  threw (verb)—past tense of *throw*, meaning to toss through the air

  through (preposition)—going into one side and out the other

- whose—who's

  whose (pronoun)—possessive case of *who*

  who's (contraction)—*who is*

- your—you're

  your (pronoun)—possessive case of *you*

  you're (contraction)—*you are*

© Gary Robert Muschla

9.1 Strange Creature

Reports of a strange creature in a lake in Scotland go back nearly two thousand years. What is the name of this creature?

To answer the question, match each word on the left with its definition on the right. Write the letter of each answer in the space above its number at the bottom of the page.

1. dessert   R. the second of two

2. accept   C. possessive form of *it*

3. country   E. very dry land

4. it's   S. leaving out

5. county   L. happening after a certain time

6. latter   H. a nation

7. its   M. to agree to

8. desert   T. food served after the main meal

9. later   N. a part of a state in the United States

10. except   O. contraction for *it is*

__ __ __ __   __ __ __ __   __ __ __ __ __ __ __
9 4 7 3   5 8 10 10   2 4 5 10 1 8 6

© Gary Robert Muschla

9.2 Around the World

This Portuguese explorer was the first man to sail around the world. Who was he?

To answer the question, match each word on the left with its definition on the right. Write the letter of each answer in the space above its number at the bottom of the page.

1. picture   N. possessive form of *you*

2. loose   F. to stop

3. lay   D. not win

4. you're   E. baseball player

5. quiet   G. to put something down

6. your   I. a drawing

7. pitcher   A. contraction for *you are*

8. lie   M. very little noise

9. quit   R. not tight

10. lose   L. to rest or recline

___ ___ ___ ___ ___ ___ ___ ___ ___   ___ ___ ___ ___ ___ ___ ___ ___
 9   7   2 10   1   6   4   6 10   5   4   3   7   8   8   4   6

Usage and Proofreading

© Gary Robert Muschla

9.3 First Football Game in the United States

The first true football game in the United States was played on November 6, 1869. Two college teams played in New Jersey. One of the teams was Rutgers. What was the other?

To answer the question, complete each sentence below. Choose your answers from the words after each sentence. Write the letter of each answer in the space above its sentence number at the bottom of the page.

1. "I love football," said Larry. "_____ my favorite sport."
   U. Its   E. It's

2. "What's _____ favorite sport?" he asked Martin.
   I. your   R. you're

3. "I think baseball is the best game in the whole _____," Martin said.
   T. country   M. county

4. "_____ the most important player on a baseball team?" asked Larry.
   J. Whose   N. Who's

5. "_____ are a lot of important players," Martin said.
   A. Their   N. There   H. They're

6. "But I think the _____ is the most important," he said.
   I. picture   C. pitcher

7. "We can watch the football game on TV," said Larry. "It has _____ started.
   I. all ready   R. already

8. "I hope my team doesn't _____," Larry said.
   I. loose   O. lose

9. "_____ the home team," he said.
   V. Their   L. There   P. They're

___ ___ ___ ___ ___ ___ ___ ___ ___
 9   7   2   4   6   1   3   8   5

© Gary Robert Muschla

9.4 The Green Earth

This scientist studies plants. What is this scientist called?

To answer the question, complete each sentence below. Choose your answers from the words after each sentence. Write the letter of each answer in the space above its sentence number at the bottom of the page.

1. "What's _____ class studying in science?" Marta asked Lauren.
   A. your   L. you're

2. "Plants," said Lauren. "_____ this week we're going to have a test."
   O. Later   I. Latter

3. "_____ is a lot of material to learn," she said.
   R. Their   N. There   L. They're

4. "Plants are found almost everywhere on earth," Lauren said, "even in _____."
   T. deserts   O. desserts

5. "They can live in most climates," she said, "_____ in extreme cold."
   N. accept   T. except

6. "Plants produce most of the oxygen that we _____," said Lauren.
   E. breath   S. breathe

7. "_____ science book is that?" asked Marta.
   B. Whose   P. Who's

8. "_____ mine," said Lauren.
   U. Its   I. It's

___ ___ ___ ___ ___ ___ ___ ___
7   2   4   1   3   8   6   5

Usage and Proofreading

© Gary Robert Muschla

Proofreading for Mistakes in Grammar

When you are proofreading to find grammar mistakes, follow the guidelines below.

1. The first word in a sentence, all proper nouns, the pronoun *I*, and all proper adjectives are capitalized.

2. All sentences have correct ending punctuation:

   • Periods for declarative and imperative sentences

   • Question marks for interrogative sentences

   • Exclamation points for exclamatory sentences

3. Commas are used:

   • To separate items in a list

   • Before conjunctions in compound sentences

   • To set off introductory words and phrases

   • Between city and state

   • To separate the day from the year in dates

   • After direct address

   • To set off quotations

4. Apostrophes are used to show possessive nouns and to show the letters left out in contractions.

5. Colons are used for time and to set off a list.

6. Hyphens are used to connect some compound words and to break words into syllables.

(continued)

© Gary Robert Muschla

Proofreading for Mistakes in Grammar (continued)

7. Quotation marks are used:

- For the titles of stories, songs, and poems

- For the chapters of books

- For the direct words of speakers

8. Italics are used:

- For the titles of books, TV shows, movies, and plays

- For the names of newspapers and magazines

9. Subjects agree with their verbs.

10. Subject, object, and possessive pronouns are used correctly.

11. The tenses of verbs are correct.

12. All words are used correctly.

© Gary Robert Muschla

9.5 Bug-Eating Mammal

This scaly, short-legged mammal lives in parts of Africa and Asia. It comes out at night and catches bugs with a sticky two-foot-long tongue. What is this animal's name?

To answer the question, read each sentence below. Find the sentence's grammatical mistake. There is no more than *one* mistake in each sentence. Choose your answers from the choices listed after the sentences. Write the letter of each answer in the space above its sentence number at the bottom of the page. If there are no mistakes, write the letter for *correct*. Not all of the answers will be used.

1. Many strange creatures' live on our planet.

2. Some animals live on the land but others live in water.

3. Elephants live in Africa and Asia, the world's biggest Continents.

4. Polar bears live in the Arctic.

5. Do you know if polar bears live in Antarctica.

6. "No, said Jessica. Polar bears don't live in Antarctica.

7. "I watched a TV show titled Bears of the North last night," Robert said.

8. "It was on at eight PM.," he said.

Answers

I. Capitalization	G. Period	L. Question Mark
O. Comma	N. Apostrophe	U. Colon
P. Italics	A. Correct	N. Quotation Marks

$\overline{}$ $\overline{}$ $\overline{}$ $\overline{}$ $\overline{}$ $\overline{}$ $\overline{}$ $\overline{}$
 7   4   1   8   2   5   3   6

© Gary Robert Muschla

9.6 Meet the Flintstones

Just about everybody knows the Flintstones. Fred and Barney were members of the Loyal Order of the Water Buffaloes. What was the title of this group's leader?

To answer the question, read each sentence below. Find the sentence's grammatical mistake. There is no more than *one* mistake in each sentence. Choose your answers from the choices listed after the sentences. Write the letter of each answer in the space above its sentence number at the bottom of the page. If there are no mistakes, write the letter for *correct*. You will need to divide the letters into words.

1. Most americans have heard of the Flintstones.

2. The Flintstones are cartoon characters, and they live in the Stone Age.

3. Fred, Wilma, Barney, and Betty is cartoon stars.

4. They starred in a TV show called The Flintstones.

5. Fred, and Wilma had a daughter named Pebbles.

6. They also had a pet named "Dino."

7. I wonder if they had any other pets?

8. The original TV series runs for six years.

9. The Flintstones are one of the worlds favorite cartoon families.

Answers

N. Capitalization	G. Verb Tense	D. Question Mark
A. Comma	O. Apostrophe	B. Subject-Verb Agreement
P. Italics	R. Correct	H. Quotation Marks

___ ___ ___ ___ ___   ___ ___ ___ ___ - ___ ___ ___
 8   2   5   1   7   4   9   9   6   3   5   6

© Gary Robert Muschla

9.7 One of Science's Greats

This Englishman was one of the world's greatest scientists. He lived about 350 years ago. Who was he?

To answer the question, read each sentence below. Find the sentence's grammatical mistake. There is no more than *one* mistake in each sentence. Choose your answers from the choices listed after the sentences. Write the letter of each answer in the space above its sentence number at the bottom of the page. If there are no mistakes, write the letter for *correct*.

1. Michael's *report* was about a famous scientist.

2. Many great discoveries were made in the past.

3. "Who is your report about," Brittany asked.

4. Michael told her, and she smiled

5. "Thats the man I'm writing about, too," she said.

6. "He was one of the greatest scientists of all time, Michael said."

7. "Yes," said Brittany. "He was born in england in 1643."

8. He dies in 1727.

9. One of his most important discoveries were about gravity.

Answers

W. Capitalization	S. Period	E. Question Mark
N. Verb Tense	T. Apostrophe	A. Quotation Marks
O. Italics	C. Correct	I. Subject-Verb Agreement

9	4	6	6	2		8	3	7	5	1	8

© Gary Robert Muschla

9.8 Arbor Day

In 1872, Julius Sterling Morton organized the first Arbor Day. In what state did the first Arbor Day take place?

To answer the question, read each sentence below. Find the sentence's grammatical mistake. There is no more than *one* mistake in each sentence. Choose your answers from the choices listed after the sentences. Write the letter of each answer in the space above its sentence number at the bottom of the page. If there are no mistakes, write the letter for *correct*. Not all of the answers will be used.

1. Julius Sterling Morton was born on April 22, 1832 in Adams New York.

2. Mortons' family moved west, and he was raised in Detroit.

3. He went to the University Of Michigan.

4. Morton was a newspaper editor, farmer, and politician.

5. Amanda said, Julius Sterling Morton founded Arbor Day.

6. "Arbor Day is a day for planting trees," she said

7. The first Arbor Day is on April 10, 1872.

8. Today, all fifty states has an Arbor Day.

Answers

A. Capitalization	K. Period	B. Subject-Verb Agreement
S. Comma	R. Apostrophe	E. Quotation Marks
O. Italics	A. Correct	N. Verb Tense

$\overline{}$ $\overline{}$ $\overline{}$ $\overline{}$ $\overline{}$ $\overline{}$ $\overline{}$ $\overline{}$
  7   5   8   2   3   1   6   4

© Gary Robert Muschla

9.9 Early Colonist

This woman was the first woman to start a town in the New World. Who was she?

To answer the question, read each sentence below. If the sentence is grammatically correct, write the letter for *correct* in the space above its number at the bottom of the page. If the sentence has a mistake, write the letter for *incorrect*.

1. This woman founded the town of Gravesend.
   A. Correct   E. Incorrect

2. Gravesend was a part of New Amsterdam.
   M. Correct   E. Incorrect

3. The Dutch founded New Amsterdam in 1625
   E. Correct   R. Incorrect

4. "Didn't the English take control of New Amsterdam in 1664," asked Peter.
   A. Correct   E. Incorrect

5. "Yes," said Laurie, "They renamed it New York."
   I. Correct   H. Incorrect

6. The city of New York grew quickly.
   Y. Correct   S. Incorrect

7. Soon New York became an important city.
   B. Correct   T. Incorrect

8. Today New York is one of the worlds greatest cities.
   E. Correct   D. Incorrect

9. "I would like to visit New York, said Peter."
   I. Correct   O. Incorrect

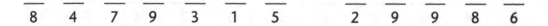

__ __ __ __ __ __ __   __ __ __ __ __
8 4 7 9 3 1 5   2 9 9 8 6

© Gary Robert Muschla

9.10 Father's Day

The first Father's Day in the United States was celebrated on June 9, 1910. But it was celebrated in only one state. What state was this?

To answer the question, read each sentence below. If the sentence is grammatically correct, write the letter for *correct* in the space above its number at the bottom of the page. If the sentence has a mistake, write the letter for *incorrect*.

1. In 1909, Sonora Smart Dodd wanted to honor her father.
   S. Correct   K. Incorrect

2. Sonoras mother had died, and her father had raised the children.
   S. Correct   T. Incorrect

3. Her father had been born in June.
   I. Correct   N. Incorrect

4. Sonora picked June for Father's Day.
   A. Correct   E. Incorrect

5. Soon other towns, and cities began to celebrate Father's Day.
   R. Correct   G. Incorrect

6. In 1924, President Calvin Coolidge made the third sunday in June Father's Day.
   I. Correct   O. Incorrect

7. In 1966, Father's Day became a national holiday.
   H. Correct   A. Incorrect

8. People throughout the United States honor they're fathers on Father's Day.
   A. Correct   W. Incorrect

9. Every year our family celebrates Father's Day.
   N. Correct   S. Incorrect

___ ___ ___ ___ ___ ___ ___ ___ ___ ___
 8   4   1   7   3   9   5   2   6   9

© Gary Robert Muschla

9.11 Tallest Mountain

At 29,078 feet, Mount Everest is the tallest mountain on earth. What mountain range is Mount Everest a part of?

To answer the question, read each sentence below. If the sentence is grammatically correct, write the letter for *correct* in the space above its number at the bottom of the page. If the sentence has a mistake, write the letter for *incorrect*.

1. Mount Everest is a part of a mountain chain in asia.
   U. Correct   A. Incorrect

2. Mount Everest is the highest mountain in the world.
   A. Correct   I. Incorrect

3. The conditions at the peak is very dangerous.
   E. Correct   A. Incorrect

4. Climbers struggle against bitter cold, powerful winds, and thin air.
   I. Correct   E. Incorrect

5. Do you know how many people have tried to climb Mount Everest.
   C. Correct   L. Incorrect

6. Many men died in avalanches, and storms.
   K. Correct   M. Incorrect

7. The top was finally reached on May 29 1953.
   N. Correct   S. Incorrect

8. Sir Edmund Hillary, an Englishman led the expedition.
   C. Correct   H. Incorrect

9. Other expeditions have climbed Mount Everest successfully.
   Y. Correct   M. Incorrect

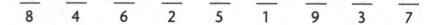

— — — — — — — — —
8   4   6   2   5   1   9   3   7

© Gary Robert Muschla

Usage and Proofreading

9.12 Cool Idea

In 1911, this man invented air-conditioning. Who was he?

To answer the question, read each sentence below. If the sentence is grammatically correct, write the letter for *correct* in the space above its number at the bottom of the page. If the sentence has a mistake, write the letter for *incorrect*.

1. The air conditioner in Jasmine's home wasn't working.
   S. Correct   K. Incorrect

2. "Its going to be a hot day," said her mother.
   E. Correct   A. Incorrect

3. "When will the repairman come," Jasmine asked?
   U. Correct   E. Incorrect

4. "Soon I hope," her mother said, "It's very warm in here."
   T. Correct   W. Incorrect

5. "Hurray!" Jasmine said when the truck pulled into the driveway.
   R. Correct   N. Incorrect

6. "I'll have the air-conditioning working in a little while," the man said.
   C. Correct   M. Incorrect

7. "I can't wait," said Jasmine.
   L. Correct   O. Incorrect

8. "Why don't you watch a movie while your waiting?" said her mother.
   A. Correct   R. Incorrect

9. Jasmine decided to watch a movie called "Ice Age."
   T. Correct   I. Incorrect

$$\overline{}\ \overline{}\ \overline{}\ \overline{}\ \overline{}\ \overline{}\qquad \overline{}\ \overline{}\ \overline{}\ \overline{}\ \overline{}\ \overline{}\ \overline{}$$

4 9 7 7 9 1   6 2 8 8 9 3 5

Usage and Proofreading

© Gary Robert Muschla

9.13 Basics of English

These are the basics of English speaking and writing. What are they?

To answer the question, read each sentence below. Decide if the statement is true or false. If it is true, write the letter for *true* in the space above the sentence number at the bottom of the page. If it is false, write the letter for *false*. You will need to divide the letters into words.

1. A noun can only name a person, animal, or place.
   C. True   T. False

2. A proper noun names only people.
   U. True   R. False

3. A proper noun always starts with a capital letter.
   C. True   E. False

4. Only action words are verbs.
   M. True   O. False

5. An adjective can modify nouns or verbs.
   T. True   N. False

6. An adverb can modify verbs, adjectives, or other adverbs.
   E. True   C. False

7. A conjunction connects words, groups of words, or sentences.
   D. True   A. False

8. A prepositional phrase always has a preposition and an object.
   W. True   N. False

9. Plural nouns always have an apostrophe.
   H. True   S. False

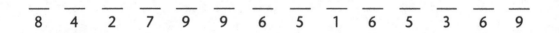

‾‾ ‾‾ ‾‾ ‾‾ ‾‾ ‾‾ ‾‾ ‾‾ ‾‾ ‾‾ ‾‾ ‾‾ ‾‾ ‾‾
 8 4 2 7 9 9 6 5 1 6 5 3 6 9

© Gary Robert Muschla

Usage and Proofreading

9.14 A Puzzle About You

If you get all of the following right, you will learn something about yourself. What are you?

To answer the question, read each sentence below and decide if the statement is true or false. If it is true, write the letter for *true* in the space above the sentence number at the bottom of the page. If it is false, write the letter for *false*. You will need to divide the letters into words.

1. Eight different kinds of words, called parts of speech, make up English.
   W. True   I. False

2. A declarative sentence asks a question.
   W. True   G. False

3. An interrogative sentence gives an order.
   O. True   I. False

4. An imperative sentence always ends with an exclamation point.
   S. True   A. False

5. In some sentences, the complete subject and the simple subject are the same.
   Z. True   N. False

6. A simple predicate is a verb or verb phrase.
   H. True   A. False

7. A complete sentence must have a subject and a predicate.
   R. True   D. False

8. Only declarative sentences end with a period.
   T. True   M. False

__ __ __ __ __ __ __ __ __ __ __ __
4   2   7   4   8   8   4   7   1   6   3   5

Usage and Proofreading

© Gary Robert Muschla

Answer Key

The answers for the worksheets contain the letters of the correct answers for individual items and the answers to the questions at the beginning of each worksheet. For those activities in which you must read a paragraph as you complete the worksheet, the entire paragraph is shown in the answer key, with the correct answers highlighted in bold. For activities in which you must identify a specific word and letter, both the word and letter are included.

Part 1

1.1   1. N 2. R 3. W 4. S 5. B 6. K 7. L 8. O 9. Y
Elwyn Brooks

1.2   1. S 2. E 3. A 4. I 5. O 6. L 7. N 8. D 9. R 10. H
Rhode Island

1.3   1. E 2. A 3. N 4. J 5. M 6. I 7. O 8. S 9. M 10. E
Mae Jemison

1.4   1. S 2. H 3. D 4. E 5. L 6. R 7. T 8. V 9. O
Theodore Roosevelt

1.5   1. E 2. O 3. S 4. A 5. W 6. M 7. N 8. J 9. T
Jamestown

1.6   1. O 2. A 3. H 4. E 5. U 6. D 7. S 8. N 9. T
ten thousand

1.7   The <u>South</u> Pole is in <u>Antarctica</u>. <u>Antarctica</u> is the <u>fifth</u> largest <u>continent</u> on the
              R   T   I   H   E
Earth. <u>It</u> is a <u>cold</u>, barren land. <u>Thick</u> ice covers most of Antarctica. <u>Even</u> in the
       C   O   M H   N
<u>summer</u>, <u>Antarctica</u> is extremely cold. <u>Only</u> a few <u>plants</u> grow in small ice-free spots far
    U   A   I   R   T

from the South Pole. The <u>temperature</u> on the <u>continent</u> is too cold for trees. <u>Penguins</u> are

                    D   **S**   **B**

the <u>most</u> numerous <u>animals</u> in Antarctica. <u>Other</u> <u>animals</u> live in the <u>oceans</u> around the

      P   **J**   **O**   **Y**   **V**

continent. The <u>first</u> <u>explorers</u> did not reach Antarctica until the 1800s. <u>Today</u>, <u>scientists</u>

            N   **R**   **S**   **D**

carry out <u>research</u> in this icy land.

         N

Richard Byrd

1.8   1. A 2. J 3. E 4. C 5. W 6. A 7. A 8. A 9. S
Sacajawea

1.9   Wilbur and Orville Wright were <u>brothers</u>. At one <u>time</u> they <u>repaired</u> bicycles.

                J   **K**   **S**   **O**   **I**

    But <u>they</u> <u>wanted</u> to fly. <u>First</u> they <u>built</u> gliders. A glider is an <u>aircraft</u> <u>without</u> an engine.

             H   **T**   **S**   **T**   **Y**   **T**   **J**

    It <u>glides</u> <u>with</u> the wind. The Wright brothers <u>learned</u> much about <u>flying</u> from their

      H   **O**   **A**   **L**

    gliders. Next, they <u>designed</u> a <u>plane</u> with a propeller. In 1903, Orville <u>made</u> the first

                          W   **R**   **K**

    <u>powered</u> airplane flight.

      N

Kitty Hawk

1.10   1. A 2. S 3. I 4. A 5. I 6. O 7. N 8. L 9. U
Louisiana

1.11   1. H 2. R 3. C 4. T 5. B 6. K 7. L 8. A 9. E
leatherback

1.12   1. O 2. S 3. E 4. S 5. Y 6. T 7. R 8. B 9. S
Betsy Ross

1.13   1. B 2. L 3. K 4. E 5. O 6. A 7. N 8. S
Lebanon, Kansas

1.14   1. S 2. C 3. E 4. T 5. A 6. H 7. W 8. V 9. T
watches TV

1.15   1. T 2. S 3. I 4. M 5. A 6. O 7. U 8. H 9. P
hippopotamus

1.16   1. W 2. F 3. H 4. D 5. T 6. E 7. S 8. R 9. O
Sherwood Forest

1.17   1. I 2. E 3. P 4. T 5. R 6. N 7. S 8. L
Splinter

1.18   1. I 2. R 3. K 4. L 5. Y 6. H 7. D 8. O 9. C
Old Hickory

1.19 1. M 2. N 3. H 4. W 5. A 6. S 7. O 8. T
Thomas Watson

1.20 1. B 2. U 3. C 4. S 5. O 6. H 7. L 8. B 9. Y
Lucy Hobbs

1.21 1. S 2. R 3. M 4. I 5. O 6. E 7. D 8. A 9. C
ice cream soda

Part 2

2.1 1. E 2. E 3. N 4. L 5. O 6. N 7. A 8. B 9. D 10. I 11. O
Daniel Boone

2.2 1. R 2. I 3. C 4. N 5. A 6. O 7. G 8. K 9. B
king cobra

2.3 1. O 2. T 3. R 4. M 5. U 6. I 7. E 8. N 9. S
Tennessee, Missouri

2.4 1. S 2. A 3. E 4. T 5. G 6. W 7. N 8. C 9. O
Conestoga wagon

2.5 1. N 2. O 3. H 4. O 5. N 6. K 7. C 8. H 9. A 10. J 11. C
John Hancock

2.6 1. T 2. F 3. E 4. N 5. G 6. I 7. L 8. M 9. O 10. R
Joseph and Jacques Montgolfier

2.7 1. A 2. T 3. E 4. E 5. T 6. H 7. C 8. I 9. L 10. W 11. S
White Castle

2.8 1. S 2. R 3. H 4. O 5. M 6. A 7. A 8. H 9. T 10. T 11. A 12. M
Thomas, Martha

2.9 1. N 2. I 3. U 4. E 5. M 6. H 7. B 8. R 9. T 10. A
Harriet Tubman

2.10 1. S 2. E 3. T 4. H 5. N 6. O 7. U 8. M 9. R
Mount Rushmore

2.11 Pluto is a dwarf planet in our solar system. Some astronomers believe that Pluto
     P H   E   A   R   S
was once a moon of Neptune. Neptune is the eighth planet from the sun. Pluto is named
        C   I   W
after the Roman god of the underworld. Pluto is small, cold, and lifeless. It can only be
          V   A   J T   K   S

seen through powerful telescopes. Astronomers think that Pluto's surface is made of
                     L   **R**   **L**

frozen gases, ice, and rock. It will be a long time before any humans visit this far-off
 P   **O**   **W**   **E**   **M** **L**   **L**   **S**

world.

Percival Lowell

2.12   1. E 2. O 3. U 4. I 5. L 6. F 7. S 8. S 9. S 10. F 11. L

fossil fuels

2.13   1. C 2. S 3. R 4. E 5. A 6. U 7. S 8. Y

Syracuse

2.14   1. N 2. N 3. A 4. A 5. Y 6. D 7. C 8. D 9. L

Candy Land

Part 3

3.1   1. N 2. E 3. O 4. A 5. Y 6. M 7. N 8. L 9. L 10. A 11. D

Pamela Lyndon

3.2   1. R 2. A 3. S 4. O 5. L 6. T 7. B 8. A 9. S

albatross

3.3   1. T 2. O 3. I 4. L 5. S 6. P 7. H 8. A

hospital

3.4   1. D (is filled) 2. I (have studied) 3. E (were puzzled) 4. G (would imagine) 5. S (can see) 6. W (are known) 7. A (may have) 8. N (might confuse) 9. T (will twinkle) 10. R (will travel)

wandering star

3.5   For thousands of years, people have dreamed of exploring space. But spaceflight
                                      S

was impossible. This finally changed in 1957. That year the first satellite was sent into
    E   **X**   **P**

space. The satellite stayed in space for twenty-one days. This satellite was followed by
                    R   **U**

others. Both the Soviet Union and the United States launched many satellites. By the
                                           V

mid-1960s, scientists had learned much about space. Many humans had flown in space.
                         T   **N**

The United States hoped to land astronauts on the moon. This would be a great
                    O   **I**

achievement. Finally, on July 20, 1969, American astronauts landed on the moon.
                                                R

Travel to another world had been achieved. Space was now the new frontier.
                               K   **S**

Sputnik

3.6 1. U 2. O 3. L 4. A 5. R 6. C 7. N 8. T 9. N
nocturnal

3.7 1. E 2. O 3. U 4. R 5. A 6. S 7. P 8. W 9. T
waterspout

3.8 1. E 2. O 3. T 4. A 5. F 6. M 7. N 8. D 9. R 10. Y
Morty and Ferdy

3.9 1. W 2. O 3. N 4. T 5. L 6. I 7. I 8. M 9. L 10. O
two million

3.10 1. H 2. N 3. O 4. S 5. Y 6. O 7. T 8. P
typhoons

3.11 1. I 2. L 3. R 4. E 5. S 6. G 7. M 8. T 9. O
meteorologist

3.12 1. L (people) 2. S (show) 3. I (wire) 4. N (hands) 5. F (performance) 6. A (applause)
7. B (bouquet) 8. M (smile) 9. T (act) 10. U (circus)
funambulist

3.13 1. E 2. A 3. I 4. L 5. T 6. P 7. O 8. H 9. C
chocolate chip

3.14 1. R 2. S 3. V 4. M 5. O 6. P 7. A 8. U 9. I 10. E 11. C 12. G
Amerigo Vespucci

3.15 1. M 2. E 3. L 4. T 5. G 6. I 7. O 8. S
seismologist

3.16 1. E 2. Y 3. N 4. I 5. T 6. O 7. P 8. H 9. S
photosynthesis

3.17 1. H 2. B 3. I 4. A 5. G 6. T 7. E 8. R
the Great Barrier Reef

3.18 1. O 2. A 3. N 4. D 5. H 6. R 7. T 8. G 9. E
great horned owl

3.19 1. E 2. L 3. L 4. B 5. O 6. Y 7. L 8. A 9. L 10. V
volleyball

3.20 1. N 2. O 3. A 4. L 5. I 6. B 7. L 8. L 9. E
Elaine Lobl

3.21 1. A 2. S 3. I 4. I 5. N 6. L 7. S 8. L 9. D 10. E 11. L
Ellis Island

3.22 1. C 2. I 3. L 4. F 5. H 6. R 7. T 8. P 9. N 10. A 11. E
African elephant

3.23 1. L 2. R 3. W 4. A 5. E 6. I 7. D 8. N
Edwin E. Aldrin

3.24 1. I 2. U 3. H 4. A 5. U 6. H 7. H 8. C 9. A
Chihuahua

3.25 1. N 2. U 3. T 4. E 5. B 6. O 7. R 8. Y 9. A
about one year

3.26 About 1,200 years ago, warriors from northern Europe sailed southward. They
_____
P

came from the countries of Denmark, Norway, and Sweden. Today, these countries
_____
I

are called Scandinavia. The warriors were fearless sailors. At first they raided the
_____   ____   _____   _____
V   I   S   K

coasts of Europe. Then some of them sailed westward. They discovered Iceland and
                                     _____   _____
                                          U   I

Greenland. They even reached North America. This was about 500 years before
                     _____   ____
                        N   E

Columbus. Their adventures were told in stories. These stories are known as sagas.
                              ____   _____
                               G   S

Vikings

3.27 1. K 2. G 3. P 4. L 5. H 6. O 7. J 8. F
FGH JKL OP

3.28 1. W 2. T 3. C 4. O 5. H 6. N 7. E 8. A 9. F 10. R
Father of New France

3.29 1. H 2. T 3. A 4. O 5. I 6. C 7. N
Cincinnati, Ohio

Part 4

4.1 1. T 2. D 3. C 4. I 5. S 6. H 7. R 8. E 9. A 10. N
Hans Christian Andersen

4.2 1. R 2. J 3. U 4. S 5. P 6. C 7. L 8. H 9. A 10. E
Charles Pajeau

4.3 1. G 2. C 3. E 4. N 5. U 6. A 7. H 8. S 9. D
Dachshund Sausages

4.4 1. A 2. O 3. I 4. R 5. D 6. L 7. F
Florida

4.5 Saturday afternoon was rainy. Serena and her friends were disappointed. They
<u>C</u> (under "her") <u>S</u> (under "They")

had planned to play soccer.

Jason looked out the window at the rain. He frowned. There seemed to be little
<u>C</u> (under "He")

for them to do.
<u>H</u> (under "them")

"What can we do?" said Serena.
<u>R</u> (under "we")

"I don't know," said Jason, shaking his head.
<u>A</u> (under "I")   <u>E</u> (under "his")

"Do you have a new CD?" he asked her.
<u>B</u> (under "you")   <u>T</u> (under "her")

"Yes," she told them. "We can listen to music."
<u>B</u> (under "she") <u>R</u> (under "them") <u>L</u> (under "We")

"That sounds like a good idea to me," Meg said.
<u>U</u> (under "me")

They listened to music for the rest of the day.
<u>E</u> (under "They")

Scrabble

4.6 Jordan and his father like hiking. Last week, for the first time, they took Jordan's
<u>O</u> (under "his")   <u>N</u> (under "they")

younger sister Shiloh with them. They packed their lunches and plenty of water.
<u>S</u> (under "them") <u>U</u> (under "They") <u>N</u> (under "their")

Shiloh helped Jordan load the car. She handed a knapsack to him. Jordan
<u>I</u> (under "him")

placed it in the trunk.
<u>X</u> (under "it")

"Here," his father said to Jordan. "This is for you."
<u>E</u> (under "his")   <u>F</u> (under "you")

He handed Jordan a compass.
<u>O</u> (under "He")

"You will have to keep us heading in the right direction," he said.
<u>R</u> (under "You") <u>E</u> (under "us")   <u>M</u> (under "he")

"What about me?" asked Shiloh. "What can I do?"
<u>E</u> (under "me")   <u>S</u> (under "I")

"You can help, too," their father said. He gave a compass to her.
<u>J</u> (under "You") <u>P</u> (under "their")   <u>T</u> (under "her")

six feet

4.7 1. A 2. E 3. W 4. E 5. L 6. L 7. U 8. B 9. H
blue whale

4.8 1. S 2. I 3. I 4. G 5. B 6. N 7. S 8. L
siblings

4.9 1. D 2. I 3. L 4. H 5. S 6. R 7. T 8. E 9. G 10. O
Theodor Seuss Geisel

4.10 1. E 2. I 3. R 4. A 5. F 6. H 7. O 8. T 9. L 10. S
sailors of the stars

4.11 1. L 2. V 3. G 4. B 5. N 6. E 7. R 8. I 9. I
Irving Berlin

4.12 1. H 2. K 3. O 4. A 5. R 6. D 7. T 8. N
North Dakota

4.13 1. N 2. A 3. D 4. E 5. V 6. I 7. O 8. G 9. C 10. L
Calvin Coolidge

4.14 1. C 2. N 3. L 4. E 5. I 6. L 7. I 8. P 9. N 10. I
penicillin

4.15 1. S (members) 2. E (Eddie) 3. T (mother) 4. A (father) 5. L (Liz) 6. N (aunt)
7. H (Happy) 8. P (Grandpa) 9. E (people)
elephants

4.16 1. A 2. A 3. C 4. R 5. D 6. A 7. U 8. B 9. R
barracuda

4.17 1. L 2. M 3. A 4. B 5. E 6. U 7. T 8. E 9. B 10. B 11. E 12. B
bumblebee bat

4.18 1. I 2. E 3. S 4. R 5. T 6. C 7. C 8. K
crickets

Part 5

5.1 1. O 2. H 3. E 4. K 5. N 6. S 7. I 8. Z 9. A 10. B 11. R 12. D
Babe Didrikson Zaharias

5.2 1. O 2. Y 3. L 4. N 5. R 6. T 7. F 8. I
fifty trillion

5.3 Deena and her <u>family</u> are going on a <u>great</u> vacation. She and her <u>younger</u> brother
                   C   A   U

can't <u>wait</u> to leave. The <u>happy</u> children <u>helped</u> their parents pack <u>big</u> suitcases. They
      L   S   M   T

planned to <u>leave</u> in the morning. They will drive <u>from</u> New York to Florida. It will be a
        I   R   H   Ā

<u>long</u> trip. Deena hopes that they <u>will</u> have <u>nice</u> weather for their vacation. Everyone is
L   N   I

looking <u>forward</u> to having a <u>wonderful</u> time.
        S   A

Australia

5.4   1. M 2. O 3. E 4. U 5. R 6. T 7. T 8. R 9. F 10. S
Fort Sumter

5.5   1. T 2. R 3. D 4. C 5. A 6. O 7. G 8. N 9. L 10. E 11. F
England to France

5.6   1. O 2. E 3. A 4. H 5. E 6. N 7. L 8. T 9. P 10. E
a telephone

5.7   1. O 2. D 3. H 4. A 5. N 6. F 7. S 8. I 9. L
Island of Hills

5.8   1. C (basic) 2. S (these) 3. P (simple) 4. L (several) 5. E (modern) 6. I (this) 7. B (big)
8. A (many)
Blaise Pascal

5.9   1. O 2. S 3. S 4. O 5. I 6. L 7. G 8. G 9. E 10. T
geologists

Part 6

6.1   1. N 2. E 3. T 4. S 5. W 6. I 7. X 8. O 9. U 10. R 11. H 12. D
two hundred six

6.2   1. E 2. N 3. A 4. T 5. G 6. I 7. R 8. O 9. L
Oregon Trail

6.3   Many people <u>feel</u> that bats are <u>very</u> <u>scary</u> animals. Some people have <u>always</u>
                  E   F   C   L

been <u>afraid</u> of bats. But most bats are not a <u>threat</u> to people. In fact, they are <u>helpful</u>.
     I   M   R

Bats hunt at <u>night</u>. They streak <u>smoothly</u> and <u>silently</u> <u>through</u> the darkness in search of
            I   Y   I   T

prey. <u>Most</u> bats eat insects. This <u>greatly</u> <u>reduces</u> the insect population. In the <u>early</u>
      N   N   R   N

morning bats <u>finally</u> <u>return</u> to their roosts.
              G   S

flying

6.4   1. T 2. P 3. H 4. U 5. S 6. E 7. A 8. L 9. R 10. C
Charles Perrault

6.5   1. O 2. R 3. M 4. P 5. D 6. A 7. C 8. L 9. E
camel leopard

6.6   1. U 2. U 3. P 4. M 5. Y 6. P 7. P 8. D
mud puppy

6.7 1. N 2. E 3. A 4. M 5. R 6. I 7. S 8. L 9. G 10. O 11. T
gila monster

6.8 1. D 2. S 3. O 4. A 5. E 6. P 7. H 8. R 9. T 10. G
the Great Red Spot

6.9 1. A (always) 2. R (recently) 3. E (very) 4. I (curiously) 5. U (carefully) 6. O (soon)
7. S (slowly) 8. P (happily) 9. L (clearly) 10. T (often)
Louis Pasteur

6.10 1. S (more easily) 2. N (most often) 3. W (most slowly) 4. I (earlier) 5. H (hardest)
6. T (fastest) 7. L (more quickly) 8. E (more carefully)
The Wise Little Hen

6.11 1. E 2. I 3. D 4. T 5. A 6. S 7. R 8. N 9. B
Saint Bernard

Part 7

7.1 1. S 2. O 3. R 4. N 5. K 6. I 7. L 8. B 9. Z 10. M 11. A
Alabama, Alaska, Arizona

7.2 Insects are found all around the world. They live in forests, fields, and deserts.
P L S I R
They live just about everywhere. They are even inside your home. Some insects are
A L D K Y
destructive. They eat crops and cause damage to homes. Some cause disease. But others
M W
are helpful. Honeybees help spread pollen among flowers. This helps the flowers bloom.
T U O T
Other insects eat harmful bugs. Insects are an important form of life on our planet.
J I W R M S
silkworm

7.3 1. I 2. E 3. I 4. S 5. N 6. P 7. D 8. P 9. N
pinnipeds

7.4 1. N 2. C 3. I 4. F 5. R 6. E 7. A 8. O
Air Force One

7.5 1. A (of your heart) 2. O (into four parts) 3. U (throughout your body) 4. I (during sleep) 5. L (to your cells) 6. R (in your lungs) 7. T (about seventy times) 8. Y (for your heart) 9. C (during exercise)
circulatory

7.6 1. X 2. O 3. R 4. N 5. P 6. E 7. S 8. Y
Pony Express

7.7   1. R (friends) 2. O (school) 3. U (Saturday) 4. D (Sunday) 5. W (week) 6. C (camp)
7. P (practice) 8. L (family)
World Cup

7.8   1. T 2. A 3. C 4. D 5. O 6. S 7. N 8. L
Scotland

7.9   1. A 2. E 3. R 4. T 5. N 6. W 7. M 8. G 9. O
Motorwagen

7.10   1. H (hey) 2. T (great) 3. I (terrific) 4. C (watch out) 5. U (ugh) 6. S (oops) 7. A (aha)
8. R (good grief)
Aristarchus

7.11   1. A 2. U 3. I 4. E 5. S 6. L 7. P 8. G 9. Z 10. W 11. J 12. Z
jigsaw puzzle

7.12   1. M 2. N 3. I 4. L 5. E 6. G 7. S 8. T 9. O
entomologist

7.13   1. H 2. P 3. S 4. T 5. D 6. A 7. R 8. O
arthropods

7.14   1. R 2. L 3. N 4. S 5. A 6. Y 7. O 8. W
Oslo, Norway

Part 8

8.1   1. R 2. N 3. O 4. H 5. E 6. U 7. M 8. R 9. D 10. S 11. T
thunderstorms

8.2   1. A (road) 2. I (captain) 3. E (senior) 4. R (Saturday) 5. U (February) 6. N (governor)
7. N (avenue) 8. N (Wednesday) 9. A (Friday) 10. R (junior) 11. V (boulevard)
12. M (September) 13. T (August) 14. B (October)
Martin Van Buren

8.3   1. U 2. H 3. J 4. C 5. E 6. B 7. M 8. N 9. S 10. A
James Buchanan

8.4   1. N 2. U 3. W 4. L 5. I 6. E 7. D 8. H 9. B
Edwin Hubble

8.5   1. O 2. I 3. H 4. F 5. G 6. D 7. T 8. S 9. R 10. E
Register of the Desert

8.6   1. G 2. I 3. T 4. E 5. A 6. S 7. U 8. N
Saint Augustine

8.7 1. E 2. R 3. C 4. L 5. F 6. N 7. A 8. I
Nile, Africa

8.8 1. U 2. E 3. I 4. H 5. R 6. D 7. N
nine hundred (with letters reversed)

8.9 1. A 2. A 3. I 4. H 5. D 6. O 7. R 8. F 9. K 10. L
Frida Kahlo

8.10 1. R 2. N 3. O 4. K 5. T 6. O 7. Y 8. W
Yorktown (with letters reversed)

8.11 Billy's Aunt Jane is an expert on the president's. There aren't many thing's Aunt
J   A   O   M
Jane doesn't know about our nation's leaders'. She knows all of the presidents' name's,
  H   N E   A S
their birthdays', and their home state's. She knows the years' of each man's presidency.
   M   U   G   D
Aunt Jane wrote books' about the presidents'. Billy's favorite is about George
      R   E A
Washington. The book tells about Washington's youth. Aunt Jane believes George
          M
Washington was one of our country's greatest president's.
          S   E

John Adams

8.12 1. I 2. A 3. H 4. G 5. T 6. N 7. R 8. O 9. S
shooting star

8.13 1. F 2. F 3. I 4. E 5. N 6. I 7. G 8. R 9. R 10. O
Ring of Fire

8.14 1. A 2. A 3. A 4. R 5. Y 6. U 7. P 8. G
Paraguay

8.15 1. E 2. E 3. I 4. L 5. A 6. S 7. L 8. L 9. C 10. W
Alice Wells

8.16 1. U 2. M 3. S 4. C 5. N 6. E 7. I 8. A 9. L
animalcules

8.17 1. M 2. I 3. O 4. N 5. E 6. O 7. N 8. R 9. A 10. E
Annie Moore

8.18 1. E 2. O 3. Y 4. N 5. R 6. U 7. G 8. D 9. H
greyhound (with letters reversed)

8.19 1. S 2. T 3. A 4. I 5. E 6. L 7. C 8. H 9. R
Charles Richter

8.20 1. I 2. U 3. A 4. Y 5. H 6. N 7. T 8. F 9. O
Fountain of Youth

8.21 1. R 2. C 3. T 4. N 5. A 6. D 7. E 8. P 9. I
pediatrician

8.22 1. I 2. E 3. I 4. R 5. P 6. G 7. D 8. B 9. P
Big Dipper (with letters reversed)

8.23 1. B 2. A 3. A 4. Y 5. A 6. C 7. R 8. P
Capybara

8.24 1. T 2. R 3. C 4. N 5. A 6. T 7. A 8. C 9. I 10. A
Antarctica

8.25 1. A 2. I 3. O 4. E 5. D 6. R 7. K 8. M 9. W
Widow-Maker

8.26 1. E 2. U 3. T 4. N 5. R 6. S 7. A 8. C
crustaceans

8.27 1. M 2. T 3. R 4. G 5. S 6. Y 7. A 8. N 9. P 10. I
praying mantis

8.28 1. O 2. O 3. U 4. U 5. L 6. N 7. L 8. H
Honolulu

8.29 1. R 2. U 3. T 4. Y 5. L 6. B 7. T 8. F 9. E
flutterby

8.30 1. S 2. O 3. C 4. J 5. K 6. E 7. A 8. M 9. O
James Cook

8.31 1. U 2. T 3. H 4. E 5. A 6. A 7. K 8. Q 9. E 10. R
earthquake

8.32 1. B 2. E 3. L 4. O 5. C 6. D 7. A 8. P 9. R
Pedro Cabral

8.33 1. H 2. A 3. I 4. I 5. C 6. N 7. M 8. G
Michigan

8.34 1. C (continents) 2. A (Asia) 3. N (North America) 4. O (ocean) 5. I (it)
6. E (equator) 7. A (America)
Oceania

Part 9

9.1 1. T 2. M 3. H 4. O 5. N 6. R 7. C 8. E 9. L 10. S
Loch Ness Monster

9.2 1. I 2. R 3. G 4. A 5. M 6. N 7. E 8. L 9. F 10. D
Ferdinand Magellan

9.3 1. E 2. I 3. T 4. N 5. N 6. C 7. R 8. O 9. P
Princeton

9.4 1. A 2. O 3. N 4. T 5. T 6. S 7. B 8. I
botanist

9.5 1. N 2. O 3. I 4. A 5. L 6. N 7. P 8. G
pangolin

9.6 1. N 2. R 3. B 4. P 5. A 6. H 7. D 8. G 9. O
Grand Pooh-Bah

9.7 1. O 2. C 3. E 4. S 5. T 6. A 7. W 8. N 9. I
Isaac Newton

9.8 1. S 2. R 3. A 4. A 5. E 6. K 7. N 8. B
Nebraska

9.9 1. A 2. M 3. R 4. E 5. H 6. Y 7. B 8. D 9. O
Deborah Moody

9.10 1. S 2. T 3. I 4. A 5. G 6. O 7. H 8. W 9. N
Washington

9.11 1. A 2. A 3. A 4. I 5. L 6. M 7. S 8. H 9. Y
Himalayas

9.12 1. S 2. A 3. E 4. W 5. R 6. C 7. L 8. R 9. I
Willis Carrier

9.13 1. T 2. R 3. C 4. O 5. N 6. E 7. D 8. W 9. S
words, sentences

9.14 1. W 2. G 3. I 4. A 5. Z 6. H 7. R 8. M
a grammar whiz